Baby Products

Sian Morrissey

 CONSUMERS' ASSOCIATION

Which? Books are commissioned by
Consumers' Association and published by
Which? Ltd, 2 Marylebone Road, London NW1 4DF
Email: books@which.net

Distributed by The Penguin Group:
Penguin Books Ltd, 80 Strand, London WC2R 0RL

First edition June 2002
Second edition July 2004

Copyright © 2002, 2004 Which? Ltd

British Library Cataloguing in Publication Data
A catalogue record for *Baby Products* is available from the British Library

ISBN 0 85202 989-6

For a full list of Which? books, please call 0800 252100, access our website at
www.which.net, or write to Which? Books, Freepost, PO Box 44, Hertford SG14
1SH. A selection of available titles is listed at the back of this book.

Editorial and production: Joanna Bregosz, Alethea Doran, Caroline Ellerby,
Vicky Fisher
Index: Marie Lorimer
Original cover concept by Sarah Harmer
Cover photograph by Robert Harding Picture Library

Typeset by Saxon Graphics Ltd, Derby
Printed and bound by Creative Print and Design, Wales

Contents

★ An asterisk next to the name of an organisation in the text indicates that the contact details can be found in this section.

Introduction

Becoming a parent can be an overwhelming and bewildering experience. Not only must you cope with sleep-interrupted nights and the responsibility of looking after your child but you also have to get to grips with a whole new world of products and terminology. The baby-product market is booming, amounting to around £3 billion a year in the UK, and the sheer choice can be daunting and confusing. Although you may do some of the purchasing before the birth, with many products it makes sense to wait before buying – so there will be numerous decisions to make about what your new baby needs. Faced with such information overload, even shopping for something as seemingly straightforward as a cot can be anxiety-inducing, given the multitude of styles and types available.

It is easy to make mistakes. As a new mother I didn't even know what baby wipes were – I bought a tub of 'moist wipes', which were designed for sticky fingers and no good at all for dirty bottoms. Most products are far more costly: research commissioned by American Express in 2003 suggested that new parents spend an average of £3,500 on products in their baby's first year (this includes pre-birth items such as maternity wear, but not child care costs). Needless to say, you don't want to be adding to this bill by wasting money on the wrong things. A hastily purchased pushchair that is too bulky to manoeuvre up the steps to your flat, for example, will just remain in your hallway gathering dust and taking up space.

The wide range of baby products available today may make decision-making difficult, but it also has its benefits. Forty years ago, for example, baby wipes didn't exist – and nor did baby monitors, changing bags, travel-system pushchairs, disposable nappies or travel cots. There were no car seats: people used to put their babies in carry cots on the back seat of the car. You couldn't take your pram on the bus because it didn't collapse or fold. New parents bought two dozen terry nappies for their baby, plus plastic pants, safety pins, nappy buckets and special disinfectant; the drying rack and washing line were always full of terry nappies, and preventing nappy rash was a major preoccupation. Compared with all this, modern baby products are blissfully sophisticated. Pushchairs are multi-functional, light and manageable; nappies are easy for you to deal with and comfortable for your baby, and you also have the option to 'buy green' if that is important to you. Safety standards are vastly improved, and the increased choice in a competitive market can also mean more affordability.

That said, however, the complexities of modern life – not to mention modern marketing techniques – have resulted in increasing pressure to buy a burgeoning number of 'necessary' baby products. Because we are more mobile we need equipment that is portable and convenient for travelling about. Working parents, under significant time constraints, are compelled to buy labour- and time-saving devices. And although there are stringent safety requirements for baby equipment, manufacturers still capitalise on parents' fears, marketing products on the basis of 'improved' safety and security. Then there's the 'trend' factor, with fashion-chasing retailers and a media preoccupation with what famous babies are wearing (or riding in) adding to the strain for new parents anxious to give their baby the best start in life.

This book aims to clear a path though the baby-product jungle. It is intended to help new parents – and grandparents – to make informed choices. It will help you identify the items that will work best for you and your circumstances; distinguish the essentials from the many things you can easily do without; and find the best value, with detailed advice about where to look when shopping around. The guide also tells you what you need to know about safety issues, and includes all the most recent test results on baby products carried out by *Which?* magazine. (If you are not a subscriber to *Which?* or *Which? Online*, and you wish to read these reports, copies of the magazine should be available in your local library.)

The guidance given in this book relates to generic product types, rather than specific items. The market is extremely fluid, nursery retailers change their stock more frequently than the lifespan of a book (often according to the season) and, with the exception of the *Which?* Best Buys, the examples we give are just that – they are not meant as precise recommendations. All prices and details of availability are correct at the time of going to press.

What you need when you have your first baby is common-sense advice, plus reassurance that you are doing the right thing. *Baby Products* will save you from shopping anxiety, helping you to choose the products you and your baby will be happy with. With useful tips from other parents, it provides you with the information and support you require to survive and enjoy parenthood.

Sian Morrissey

Chapter 1

Where to shop

When you first become a parent and venture into the uncharted world of baby stores and catalogues, you will be confronted with a bewildering array of equipment. It may be some comfort to know that very little of this is absolutely necessary – at least at first. Those items that are essential from birth and in the first few weeks, as well as those that are optional but may be useful, are covered in Chapter 2.

There is no shortage of retail outlets for baby products; the difficulty is more in deciding where to start. Your choice includes high-street chains and department stores, supermarkets, catalogue stores and small independent shops – as well as mail-order and online nursery specialists. Each has its strengths and weaknesses: these are outlined below, and should help to focus your shopping. If you use the Internet for making purchases, you may also find it worth visiting parenting websites for advice and information from other parents.

Baby-product shopping guide

The most familiar baby-product outlet is Mothercare, but there are many other options; some well known, others less so.

Large nursery chain stores

- **Mothercare★** is the largest and best-known nursery chain in the UK. There are branches throughout the country, and a number of large, out-of-town stores called 'Mothercare World', which have a far wider range of stock than the town-centre shops. You can get more or less everything you need at Mothercare – the range is wide and the prices reasonable, and the Mothercare own-label is especially good value. However, the store is not so good for more unusual items. You can order via the catalogue or the website, both of which offer a far more extensive range than in many of the high-street stores. You can apply for a Mothercare account card to help you spread the cost of payment.

- **Babies 'R' Us★** is the specialist baby department of the US Toys 'R' Us chain. As well as baby toys, it offers just about everything else you might need – from nursery wardrobes to wipes. The full selection won't be available in every store but can be found in the catalogue or on the website. The range is comparable to that of Mothercare and in many cases the products are slightly cheaper. The main disadvantage is that because there are far fewer stores you may not have the same opportunity to see and try out the products.
- **Mamas & Papas★** is a major nursery goods manufacturer which also has 19 Mamas & Papas Superstores around the country. You'll only be able to buy Mamas & Papas products at these stores; however, the range is reasonable.

High-street chains and supermarkets

- **Boots★** has a good reputation for feeding essentials (bottles, sterilisers and bibs, for example, as well as its own-brand baby food), in addition to nappies and baby toiletries. Larger outlets also sell a decent selection of toys. As a general rule, stores tend to stock small rather than large items of baby equipment. However, you can order a wide selection of larger items from the Boots website or from the catalogue, available in stores. At the time of writing there was a choice of 18 cots or cot beds available on the Boots website, which is comparable with the choice on offer at Mothercare.
- **Marks and Spencer★** stocks nursery items in some larger stores. You can choose from a small selection of car seats, pushchairs and cots, although M&S is stronger on baby clothes and nursery accessories such as bedding. Again, you can buy from the catalogue or online, although these don't feature all M&S baby products available and you won't find the same wide range as in the largest stores.
- **Supermarkets** are the big players in the market for baby essentials. Your nearest major supermarket will probably be one

of the best places for picking up essentials such as nappies, wipes and formula milk along with your regular shopping. Most produce their own lines, which are comparable in quality to the leading brands but better value for money. A few supermarkets have gone one step further. For example, **Sainsbury's**★ has a deal with the Early Learning Centre (ELC)★ and Adams children's clothes so a range of ELC toys and Adams baby clothes are now available in many Sainsbury's stores. **Asda**★ offers a good selection of baby and children's clothing. A selection of larger Asda Walmart stores also contain a baby department, with car seats, pushchairs and other general nursery items. Bear in mind that shopping online can be useful for nappies and groceries when you have a small baby, and all of the main supermarkets offer this service.

- **Littlewoods**★ has good-value baby clothes and its website has a reasonable range of nursery items including cots and pushchairs.
- **Woolworths** is also popular for value-for-money baby clothes, and larger branches have an excellent selection of well-known brand-name toys. Some branches will also sell baby essentials such as nappies and wipes.

Loyalty schemes

Lots of retailers try to encourage customer loyalty for their baby goods by running baby club schemes, which give you money-off coupons on a range of products. Both **Tesco**★ and **Babies 'R' Us**★, for example, give vouchers worth up to £150 if you join their clubs. Signing up also entitles you to free club magazines and mailings. Nappy manufacturers Pampers and Huggies also run their own clubs.

Department stores

Some department stores have excellent nursery departments. Although the ranges available may not be vast, many will have a good selection of quality products. It's worth paying a visit to your local department store to see what it can offer. **John Lewis**★, for example, has a particularly good reputation for 'up-market' nursery products as well as out-of-the-ordinary accessories and own-label and 'designer' baby clothes (although not all stores will stock the same items). Baby products and toys are listed on the website, and you can order online.

Catalogue stores

Although you may think of catalogue stores such as **Argos★** as the sort of place to go for a cheap video recorder or vacuum cleaner, they can also be good sources of nursery equipment. Argos in particular has outlets all over the country, and its nursery range includes most of the items you might be looking for, with major brand names represented – all at value-for-money prices. You can order at your local store, or from home via the catalogue or online. **Index★**, which is Argos's main rival, has a similar range. **Vertbaudet★**, a French catalogue company with a UK arm, also sells nursery items and has a large choice of baby and children's clothing. Catalogue companies through which you can pay for goods by instalment may be worthwhile for pricier large items of equipment. **Kays★**, for example, has a reasonable selection of nursery products and you can pay over a period of a few months.

With all catalogue and mail-order outlets, the drawback is of course that you can't check out your goods before you buy, and with items such as cots and pushchairs this is something many parents want to do.

Out-of-town stores

The large out-of-town superstores run by some of the main super-markets – Sainsbury's Savacentres, for example – often sell larger items of baby equipment as well as baby milk and food, toys, nappies and toiletries. **Ikea★** is worth a look for its range of nursery furniture – you can buy simply designed cots, changing tables, high-chairs, wardrobes and chests of drawers, as well as toddler tables, chairs and beds (and lots of other practical baby products and toys), all at reasonable prices. Well-known furniture stores such as **MFI** have children's bedroom ranges (but not cots), and you can get a fair selection of children's furnishings such as 'character' lamps and nursery wallpaper and borders at the big DIY stores such as **Homebase★** and **B&Q★**.

Another more unusual out-of-town option is the **Nippers★** chain. These are franchised nursery stores based in large farm buildings and often run by farming families. They sometimes have quite extensive ranges due to the size of the sales area (often converted barns), with on-site parking. There are a number of stores dotted around the country – see the website to find out whether there is one near you.

Independent nursery stores

Faced with intense competition from the 'big players' in the nursery goods market, small independent nursery shops may not have quite the same drawing power they had for new parents in the past. However, your local independent nursery store could be one of the best places to go for one-to-one advice in an unhurried atmosphere. If you are served by the owner/manager or an experienced assistant, you may reap the benefits of talking to someone with plenty of knowledge of a wide range of nursery items and who will be prepared to spell out the pros and cons of various lines and brands. The disadvantage is that, depending on the size of the store, you won't be able to view the same extensive range as in larger chain stores (although the shop may be able to order specific items for you). Price may also be an issue – independents won't have the 'value' own-brand lines that the main chain stores have, or the mass buying power.

You may find that your local independent nursery store is part of a small chain, such as **Lilliput**★. Bear in mind though that 'independent' doesn't necessarily mean small – there are various large independent stores with a wide selection of products. Some specialise in specific products from one or two manufacturers, so if you are keen on a certain brand, they can be a good place to look.

Many independent nursery stores also have an online presence. Look in your Yellow Pages under 'Baby Goods and Services', or Thomson Local directory under 'Baby and Nursery Equipment', to find out about nursery shops in your area, or contact the British Association of Nursery and Pram Retailers★.

> ❝I think people automatically head towards Mothercare just because it's easy and they're familiar with it, when in fact a local independent nursery store can have a more interesting range of stuff. When we were looking for a buggy board for Chloe and Mothercare proved fruitless, a friend suggested I check out a small nursery

store in town off the main high street. I had never been before but it was crammed with goodies – and I got my buggy board. I don't go there for basics, but if I want anything unusual it's the first place I try. **"**

Charlie, mother of Chloe, now 5 and Jack, 2

Mail-order and online nursery specialists

Ordering nursery items either by mail order or online certainly has its advantages. For one thing, you don't have to brave the shops with a baby in tow – you can browse the catalogues in the comfort of your home. Many of the mail-order and online nursery specialists have an interesting selection of products that you won't find in your local Mothercare or other nursery store; the products are often sourced abroad and are introduced into the UK for the first time by these companies. If you are interested in something a bit out of the ordinary or are on the lookout for innovative ideas, there's a good chance of finding something to interest you in one of the specialist catalogues.

However, there are also disadvantages with buying in this way. The most obvious one is that you won't be able to see the goods before you buy or try them out in the way you can in a shop. This is particularly relevant when it comes to larger items such as pushchairs and cots – you can't, for example, test out how easy a pushchair is to fold or how smoothly the side of a cot slides down. You won't get the one-to-one attention or the demonstration of how to use a particular item that you may be offered in a high-street nursery store (although you can often get telephone advice). This drawback, of course, also applies to buying online or via mail order from one of the chain outlets such as Mothercare – although with these, depending on the store, you can of course go and look at the items in the shop before you buy. Bear in mind you usually have to pay for delivery, which typically costs around £4.

If you decide a product isn't quite right for you or isn't what you were expecting once you have received it, you should be able to return it, but this can be a nuisance and you'll often have to pay the return postage costs. And if you associate catalogue shopping with relatively cheap prices, be warned that this doesn't necessarily apply to these nursery catalogue specialists – many have quite an up-market feel and the products they sell and prices they charge tend to reflect this.

If you're interested in buying online or by mail order, the following specialists are worth a look (some have 'real world' shops too). Some of the products available through these companies are mentioned in other chapters in this book. Other sites that deal with specific products (e.g. cloth nappies or travel equipment) are cited in the relevant chapters. See page 29 for a list of specialist online baby-clothes retailers.

- **Beaming Baby★** – products with an environmentally friendly slant, including aromatherapy baby toiletries, organic cotton cuddly toys and bed linen, reusable nappies and a small selection of 'Fair Trade' clothing.
- **Blooming Marvellous★** – maternity wear, including evening and professional outfits, plus accessories such as nursing bras, pregnancy support pillows and a device to listen to your unborn baby's heartbeat in the last few weeks; as well as nursery products and baby clothing (has eight 'real world' shops).
- **Cheeky Rascals★** – practical products, including moulded, ergonomically designed feeding equipment, a good selection of travel equipment (with a wide choice of toddler 'buggy boards'), reusable nappies and a small selection of toys.
- **The Great Little Trading Company★** – extensive range of nursery furnishings and products, plus a large selection of indoor and outdoor toys and child-sized furniture; good for products for older children as well as for babies.
- **Green Baby★** – specialises in 'natural' baby products, including reusable nappies, organic cotton clothing and bedding, and wooden items (such as a baby hairbrush and toothbrush) from sustainable sources; the range is quite limited but unusual, and there are two 'real world' shops.
- **JoJo Maman Bébé★** – maternity wear plus nursery products, baby clothing, and lots of toys and storage products (has three 'real world' shops).
- **Little Green Earthlets★** – three-wheeler pushchair and reusable nappy specialists plus nursery goods with an environmentally friendly slant, including woollen clothing,

non-endangered-species sea sponges for babies, unbleached cotton baby towels and bibs, and Merino wool blankets.

- **Mini Boden**★ – stylish and practical baby and children's clothing, up to pre-teens.
- **Urchin**★ – out-of-the-ordinary furnishings, toys and practical products (for example, the 'spotty potty', fleece blankets with your baby's name and pop-up travel cribs).
- **Kiddicare**★ – wide range of well-known brands of nursery items including pushchairs and car seats, many with good discounts.

"The nursery mail-order catalogues are lethal to a shopaholic like me. They are nice to look through and have lots of items that seem like 'really good ideas' at the time but when you order them, even though there's nothing wrong with the products as such, you don't actually use them. My 'bath toy net' has stayed in its box, the pricey Winnie-the-Pooh alarm clock has been rejected by my four-year-old, who suddenly decided Winnie-the-Pooh was babyish, and I have quite a few lovely items of children's clothing that are far too big even though the label has the right age – she'll grow into them of course but her tastes may have changed by then. Beware of impulse buying!**"**

Catherine, mother of May, age 4

Researching products using the Internet

In addition to straightforward online shopping, the Internet can be very handy if you are trying to track down a specific product, look for the best deal, or want to know how useful other parents have found a product to be.

There are a number of parenting sites with 'chat rooms' or 'discussion forums' where you can ask other parents for information on their experiences of specific products. These can be a helpful source of independent viewpoints on items before you buy. Try the following sites.

- **www.ukparents.co.uk** – this is one of the best-known and widely used parenting sites. Click on the 'Where to Find' section in the 'Noticeboards and General' forum if you're searching for a product and can't find it – other parents may be able to help. The 'Buy and Sell' forum gives parents the opportunity to buy and sell second-hand nursery equipment. There is also a 'Swaps' forum, and even a forum devoted to reusable nappies ('Cloth nappies'), with lots of advice and nappies to buy. Anyone can read the messages, but you must log in to post or reply to a message.

- **www.babyworld.co.uk** – click on the 'Discuss Products' forum to exchange views on products or ask for advice. You need to sign up as a member before you can read any messages on the forum. The site also publishes magazine-style buyers' guides, which give general advice, and there are test results on a selection of products.

You can also read product reviews and ratings by other parents on a range of nursery equipment at **ciao.co.uk**, – a shopping guide website based solely on customer reviews.

Another way to search for products on the Internet is to use a shopping directory site, or the shopping directory section of a general site (usually referred to as a 'portal' site). These sites don't usually sell products themselves but present a 'gateway' to retail sites in the area in which you are interested. **www.ukchildrens directory.com**, for example, as well as providing general information on services such as childcare, includes a 'Baby and nursery' section with an extensive list of links to retailers specialising in baby products. Many of those featured are small, independent businesses, and this can therefore be a useful way of locating more unusual products not available in the high-street shops (for example, handmade children's beds, softplay equipment and designer clothing). **www.babysurf.co.uk** has links to major manufacturers' and retailers' sites. Shopping directory sites that don't specialise in children's products will often still have a section relating to children – for example, try the 'Toys and games' section of **www.topoftheshops.co.uk** for links to a number of toy retailer websites. One slightly different directory site is **babydirectory.com** – you click on your area on a map of the UK, and a local baby directory pops up. Click on the type of product you are interested in (e.g. 'Christening gowns') for contact details of relevant local shops. Some of these local directories are more comprehensive than others, so how useful the site is will depend on where you live and your prior knowledge of baby shops in your area.

You can also use the Internet to help you shop around for the best deal on a product – particularly large items such as pushchairs and cots. Look at the sites of high-street retailers such as Boots★ and Mothercare★ for their latest deals. Some nursery-product sites make a point of claiming that they will beat any other price. Others market themselves specifically as 'cut-price' outlets – **www.discountbabystore.co.uk**, for example, says that it sells all products at up to 50 per cent discount on recommended retail prices. Bear in mind that with such deals you may not get the latest models at big discounts, but you could well find a bargain on end-of-line and past-season goods.

Another option is to try an Internet auction site. **www.ebay.co.uk** has quite an extensive 'Baby Items' section on its site, offering mostly second-hand clothes but also 'nearly new' pushchairs, nursery furniture and many other baby goods. Remember that if you are dissatisfied with the goods you buy from an auction site, because you are effectively buying from a private seller your rights are more restricted than if you buy from an online or 'bricks and mortar' store.

Second-hand baby clothes and equipment

When you have a baby, friends and relatives are usually only too pleased to pass on equipment and clothes that they no longer need. Parents who turn up their noses at hand-me-downs are missing out. Spare clothing is always useful – not until you have a baby do you realise quite how much clothing they can get through in a week or even a day. If you are offered equipment you're not sure you'll use, it's worth accepting and using it on a trial basis – you may find it indispensable or it may help to clarify what you really do need and would like to buy new.

Understandably, most parents want to buy equipment such as a pushchair or a cot, which will be in use day-in, day-out for a couple of years or so, new. However, those items with a short lifespan that can be pricey to buy new, and with which there is no guarantee that they will suit your baby's needs or foibles, are good candidates for second-hand gifts or purchases. Examples of these are baby 'play' equipment such as an automated swinging cradle or a baby bouncer (see pages 201–3). Moses baskets, cribs and carry cots can also be worth acquiring as hand-me-downs, as they will only be in use for a few months or even weeks, until your baby moves into a cot (you may want to buy a new mattress for hygiene reasons but you need to make sure it fits correctly – see pages 73–8).

Buying second-hand

Parents are usually more comfortable using second-hand equipment from a trusted source such as a friend or relative, rather than from a shop. In the case of car seats in particular (see pages 136–46), this is a sensible attitude. But second-hand stores and charity shops are worth a browse for other 'nearly new' bargains. Some independent nursery shops have second-hand sections and some deal in just second-hand goods – these can be much better places to buy from as there is a good chance that you will be dealing with a sales assistant who knows about the equipment. It is also more likely that a product's condition will be checked before it is put on sale.

Local branches of the National Childbirth Trust (NCT)★ regularly organise 'Nearly New Sales' and these can be very useful sources of cheap equipment, clothes and toys, much of which will have had quite limited use. Visit the NCT's website for lists of sales in your area or look out for adverts in local newspapers and shops. You could also try the 'Nearly New' section of **www.netmums.com**, a local information website for parents. Or browse **www.kidsgloriouskids.co.uk**, which sells mainly 'gently worn' children's clothes plus toys.

When you buy second-hand goods from a shop you have the same legal rights as when buying new. This means the goods must be fit for the purpose for which they're intended, including any purpose you made clear when purchasing, and must be of satisfactory quality. But the law also says that you must take into account the price you paid and be prepared to have lower expectations of quality than if the goods were new. You can also take goods back if there is a problem. However, buying from car boot sales, auction sites, jumble sales or through the small ads is more of a risk. The Child Accident Prevention Trust★ advises parents not to buy

Is your baby a 'bappie'?

Money may not be quite such an issue for some first-time parents these days as it was for many in the past. With the continuing trend for women to have their first baby in their thirties, these days couples are more likely to be established in their careers and have a fair amount of disposable income to spend on a baby. Babies of such parents have been dubbed 'bappies' – 'babies of affluent, professional parents'.

According to market research, one consequence of this social trend has been an increased demand for new designs of nursery equipment that complement the lifestyle of 'bappie' families. Adaptable products, such as travel-system pushchairs (see pages 176 and 177), which fit in with car-centred lifestyles, are increasingly popular. Trendy three-wheeler pushchairs, originally designed for sports enthusiasts, are bought by many parents because of their stylish looks rather than their 'off-road' capabilities. Portable products such as travel cots and highchairs are in demand for holidays. 'Designer' nursery goods labels are more numerous and more accessible to parents than ever before. Buying baby products, for some, is an enjoyable leisure activity rather than a cause for financial anxiety.

equipment from these sources. If you do, however, the important thing is to satisfy yourself as far as possible that the product is safe, by observing the following guidelines.

Wherever you get second-hand equipment from, you should check it over for damage and wear and tear. If there are no fitting or assembly instructions with a product that needs careful fitting or assembly, avoid it altogether. Bear in mind too that improvements in the safety standards and design of equipment are being made all the time, and any product you obtain second-hand may not be up to date in this respect. For more information on specific second-hand items see pages 67 and 68 on cots, page 126 on highchairs, page 142 on car seats, page 161 on travel cots and page 185 on pushchairs.

"I have long been a fan of the NCT Nearly New Sales. My spare buggy came from one (a fiver and in perfect condition) and my daughters have now got a range of 'designer' clothes I would never have bought new."

Sarah, mother of Stephanie, 5, Natalie, 3 and Phoebe, 1

Equipment for children and parents with special needs

If you have a child with special needs you may need specialised equipment that is not available from standard shops. Some equipment from mainstream manufacturers has particular uses for disabled children – for example, toilet-seat adaptors (see pages 209 and 210) are helpful for children with balance and movement difficulties, according to the Research Institute for Consumer Affairs (RICA). The Redinap★ Ezeechanger, a wall-mounted baby-changing unit (see page 89), is marketed as being helpful for parents in a wheelchair or with bending or kneeling difficulties, because it can be attached to the wall at a comfortable height for whoever is using it. The Rabbitts★ Mat (see page 40) is a changing mat that incorporates a shoulder-and-waist harness so you have both hands free when trying to change the nappy of a struggling baby – this is also marketed as being of help to parents with children with special needs and to disabled parents. The three-wheeler pushchair manufacturer, Baby Jogger, produces a special-needs version of the three-wheeler with a wider and deeper seat which is available from Kidsense UK★.

There are also many specialist retailers that cater for children with special needs. The following three organisations will be able to provide further information about these. You could also look at the furniture and equipment section of the **www.specialneedskids.co.uk** website for links to specialist retailers and manufacturers.

- **The Disabled Living Foundation★**, a charity with a particular interest in special-needs equipment, produces free and detailed factsheets on a wide range of equipment that may be useful to parents of children with special needs. Three of these factsheets – *Choosing children's daily living equipment, Choosing children's* *mobility equipment* and *Choosing children's play equipment* – are the most relevant and you can download them directly from the website or send an SAE. The website also has a discussion forum where participants exchange views or give advice on equipment.

- **Ricability**★ publishes test reports on equipment for the disabled, including children, from research carried out by the independent Research Institute for Consumer Affairs (RICA). Recent reports include ones on pushchairs and highchairs suitable for use by disabled parents. There is a discussion forum on the website, and Ricability can answer queries if you want more guidance on specific products.
- **The Disabled Living Centres Council**★ provides details of local Disabled Living Centres (there are 47 around the UK) where you can see and try out equipment and get advice on how to obtain it.

Hiring baby equipment

On some occasions you may need to hire equipment: either when on holiday, when you won't want to be over-burdened with luggage, or at home – perhaps if you have guests staying and need a spare cot, or if you know you will only be using an item (such as a baby swing) for a short time. Fortunately (particularly in holiday resorts) there are companies that hire out baby equipment, including pushchairs. If you are staying in a holiday cottage organised via a letting agent, you will normally be able to hire cots and highchairs through the company. Sometimes these will be included in the cost of the cottage. If the agent itself doesn't deal with the baby equipment you want, it may be able to put you in touch with a local company that does. For more information on products you need for travelling with your baby, including on holiday, see Chapter 5.

You may find that your local independent nursery store has a 'for hire' section. If it doesn't, it should be able to put you in touch with a company that does. You could also look in your local Yellow Pages or Thomson Local directory – try under 'Baby Goods and Services' or 'Baby and Nursery Equipment' rather than 'Hire' – if there is a specialist hire company in your area, it should be listed in this section.

Baby showers

The baby shower concept, where you hold a party for your baby either just before or after the birth and guests bring gifts, is big in the US and may appeal to you. Retailers in the UK are cottoning on to this market and some nursery specialists operate a 'baby shower gift list' (the Lilliput* chain, for example, offers this service and even supplies invitations for your guests). The principle is the same as that for a wedding present list. You choose what you want from the store and the store keeps the details on a list. Your friends and relatives can then contact the store and order what they want to give you from the list. The retailer administers the list to make sure you don't get two of the same thing. Of course, you don't need to have a formal baby shower party to make use of this kind of service – you may find it useful to simply tell anyone who asks you what you want for your new baby that you have a 'wish list' at the store and that they can choose from this.

Websites

Argos	www.argos.co.uk
Asda	www.asda.co.uk
B&Q	www.diy.com
Babies 'R' Us	www.babiesrus.co.uk
Babydirectory	www.babydirectory.com
Baby Surf	www.babysurf.co.uk
Babyworld	www.babyworld.co.uk
Beaming Baby	www.beamingbaby.com
Blooming Marvellous	www.bloomingmarvellous.co.uk
Boots	www.boots.com
Ciao	www.ciao.co.uk
Cheeky Rascals	www.cheekyrascals.co.uk
Child Accident Prevention Trust	www.capt.org.uk
Disabled Living Centres Council	www.dlcc.co.uk
Disabled Living Foundation	www.dlf.org.uk
Discount Baby Store	www.discountbabystore.co.uk

Ebay	www.ebay.co.uk
The Great Little Trading Company	www.gltc.co.uk
Green Baby	www.greenbabyco.com
Homebase	www.homebase.co.uk
Ikea	www.ikea.co.uk
Index	www.index.co.uk
John Lewis	www.johnlewis.com
JoJo Maman Bébé	www.jojomamanbebe.co.uk
Kays	www.kaysnet.com
Kiddicare	www.kiddicare.com
Kidsense	www.kidsense.co.uk
Kids Glorious Kids	www.kidsgloriouskids.co.uk
Lilliput	www.lilliput.com
Little Green Earthlets	www.earthlets.co.uk
Littlewoods	www.littlewoods.com
Mamas & Papas	www.mamasandpapas.co.uk
Marks and Spencer	www.marksandspencer.co.uk
MFI	www.mfi.co.uk
Mini Boden	www.boden.co.uk
Mothercare	www.mothercare.com
National Childbirth Trust	www.nctpregnancyandbabycare.com
Net Mums	www.netmums.com
Nippers	www.nippers.co.uk
Rabbitts	www.rabbitts.com
Redinap	www.redinap.co.uk
Ricability	www.ricability.org.uk
Sainsbury's	www.sainsburys.com
Special Needs Kids	www.specialneedskids.co.uk
Tesco	www.tesco.com
Top of the Shops	www.topoftheshops.co.uk
UK Children's Directory	www.ukchildrensdirectory.com
UKparents	www.ukparents.co.uk
Urchin	www.urchin.co.uk
Vertbaudet	www.vertbaudet.co.uk
Woolworths	www.woolworths.co.uk

Chapter 2

First essentials

Although baby magazines and retailer catalogues can make you feel that you need an endless list of items for your new baby, you really don't. You do need certain basics from day one – nappies, a few changes of clothing, a suitable place for your baby to sleep and perhaps feeding equipment – and, if you will be travelling by car, a car seat. Fairly soon you will also need a pushchair or baby carrier. Beyond this, however, what you buy is largely down to personal choice and circumstances. Some new parents feel they want to kit their baby and the nursery out in full glory from day one; others want to stick to the bare minimum, either because their finances do not allow more or because they just want to keep things simple. If you feel overwhelmed by the wealth of baby items on offer, bear in mind that with most of them it is worth waiting until after the birth and taking your time over choosing what to get. As you become used to your baby's needs, and your own priorities evolve, you will be in a better position to decide what will be useful to you and what won't.

Some essentials are covered in this chapter. Others, such as bottles and teats, are dealt with in other chapters, as indicated below.

What you need in time for the birth:

- Moses basket, cradle, carry cot or cot (see pages 63–72)
- mattress and bedding (see pages 73–86)
- clothing – four to six sleepsuits and bodysuits are sufficient to start off with, plus a couple of cardigans and a hat
- nappies – a packet of first-size disposables to start off with, or a selection of reusable nappies
- cotton wool or baby wipes

- a shawl or blanket to wrap your baby in
- bottles, formula milk and some sort of sterilising equipment (see pages 98–110) if you are bottle-feeding (it's also worth having some bottles and formula even if you are planning to breast-feed – just in case)
- car seat (see pages 136–46) if you will be travelling by car from day one (i.e. bringing your baby home from hospital).

What you will need in the first days and weeks:

- a fully reclining pushchair or pram, or a baby carrier or sling (see Chapter 6)
- a towel for just your baby's use and a gentle baby-bath solution.

Other items you may choose to buy:

- pair of scratch mittens
- changing mat or changing unit (see pages 86–90 for changing units)
- muslin cloths or bibs (see pages 129–31) for spills and possetting
- breast pads, feeding bra and possibly breast pump if you are breast-feeding (see pages 111–4)
- dummies
- bouncy cradle
- baby bath or bath supports (but the sink or main bath will do fine)
- baby monitor.

'Non-baby' items that you will probably be thankful for:

- an efficient, reliable washing machine
- a clothes-drying rack if you do not have a tumble-drier
- a microwave for sterilising and/or for heating baby food later on.

> "If you buy muslin cloths, get coloured rather than white ones – you'll be able to dig them out more easily from the piles of white-dominated washing."
>
> Kirsty, mother of Samuel, 6 months

" We spent our money on a new washing machine and left buying cots until we found cut-price ones in the sales. I use the washing machine almost every day while the cots have long since been passed on to someone else. "

Elizabeth, mother of twins Michael and Tim, age 4

Clothing

You will probably be inundated with all sorts of baby clothes from friends and relatives. It will soon become apparent that some items are more fiddly to put on your baby than others, and these will be the ones that are cast to the back of the wardrobe or brought out just for special occasions. If you are buying baby clothes yourself for a newborn, bear the following points in mind.

- Sleepsuits, which are all-in-one outfits with built-in feet, are the most practical item to dress your baby in during the early weeks. They are usually made of cotton jersey or a poly-cotton mix and are comfortable to wear and easy to wash.
- Avoid sleepsuits that have poppers at the back rather than the crotch area, otherwise every time you want to change a nappy you will have to take the whole outfit off. Any item with poppers down the back has the potential to be uncomfortable for your baby as he or she will be lying on the seam.
- Keep clothes in the 'newborn' size to a minimum, or bypass them altogether – your baby will outgrow these very quickly. Clothes labelled '0–3 months' will last for longer, although they will be on the large side at the beginning.
- Necklines of jumpers and sweatshirts should have poppers at the side so you are not pulling them over your baby's face to put them on.
- Knitted items such as hand-made cardigans and shawls should have a fine weave otherwise little fingers can get caught up in the gaps.
- You will be doing a lot of washing – some babies can go through several outfits a day – so any clothing you buy has to be suitable to wash on a reasonably hot cycle. Hand-wash- and dry-clean-only garments are definitely a bad idea, unless they are for a special occasion.

- Bodysuits, which are all-in-one vests with a wide neck and poppers at the crotch, are another newborn staple. These are more practical than standard vests as they don't ride up.

- Baby bootees can look cute but are not necessary, and knitted bootees in particular often fall off – socks are more practical.

- A snowsuit can be a useful item of clothing in winter if you are taking your baby for walks in the pram, but remember you don't need layers of blankets and clothing too. If you buy a snowsuit make sure it is easy to take off or at least undo if you spend time indoors – for example, in a warm shop. Buy it a size larger than your baby's normal clothes so that it is not too constricting.

- Clothes with European brand names tend to be smaller than equivalent-sized UK brands.

- Many retailers produce 'gift pack' sets of clothes for newborns. The chances are that these will include items that you don't use or find too fancy, so leave these packs for people to give as gifts and spend your money on more practical clothing.

> **"**Stockpile clothes for the future from the sales. We will buy clothes for even a couple of years ahead if they are a bargain. Out-of-season clothes are a good bet. And if you can, wait until the sales are well under way – some shops have excellent sales and carry on reducing stuff until the end.**"**
>
> Al, father of Maddy, 2 and Liam, 1

Scratch mittens

The skin of new babies can be very sensitive and prone to rashes, and their fingernails quite hard. The natural instinct of a baby is to scratch such irritation. Scratch mittens are simple, thin cotton mittens which help prevent your baby from damaging his or her skin by scratching. They are widely available from nursery stores, costing around £1.50 for a pack of two pairs.

Shopping for baby clothes

Buying clothes for your baby can be a real pleasure. There is an abundance of stylish baby clothes on offer, many of them at reasonable prices, and you certainly don't have to go down the designer-baby road to kit your baby out in a fashionable as well as a practical way. High-street stores including Debenhams, Next, Hennes, Baby Gap, Adams, Marks and Spencer* and Woolworths have worthwhile selections. Some of the supermarkets – particularly Asda* – have a good reputation for value-for-money children's clothes. You could also try the following online children's clothes retailers for more unusual designs – some have mail-order catalogues too. (See Chapter 1 for more general information on shopping outlets.)

- **Baby Planet*** – tie-dye, hippy-chic baby and toddler clothes.
- **Charlie Crow*** – imaginative dressing-up costumes for ages 18 months to 9 years.
- **Mini Boden*** – lots of understated but stylish and practical clothes for babies to pre-teens.
- **Mischief Kids*** – Lancashire-based shop selling designer clothes (including DKNY, Moschino and Miniman) for babies to teens.
- **Starchild*** – soft leather, brightly designed baby shoes.
- **Sunday Best*** – specialist in christening gowns, dresses and rompers.

Nappies

Packets of nappies are likely to be taking up space in your shopping trolley for years to come. If you opt for disposables – as most parents do – you will be buying them for two-and-a-half to three years from the birth of your baby. With nappies (and their contents) becoming part of your daily life for so long, you will want to make sure you are choosing the right one for your baby. Babies come in all shapes and sizes and there may be some trial and error involved in finding a nappy you are happy with. The question of disposables versus washables is addressed later in this section (see pages 35–7).

Disposable nappies

Modern disposable nappies work well at absorbing liquid because they contain a highly absorbent material, called polyacrylate (if you cut open a nappy, you'll see the polyacrylate material has the texture of compressed cotton wool). This is trapped inside the nappy layers and can absorb many times its own weight in liquid. When the polyacrylate gets wet it turns into gel, holding in the wetness in the process (if a wet nappy splits, the gel is clearly visible).

Kimberly-Clark, maker of Huggies, and Proctor & Gamble, maker of Pampers, are the main manufacturers of disposables; you will find these brands almost everywhere. Most supermarkets also produce own-brand nappies. Nappies come in a range of sizes, from tiny ones for premature or low-birthweight babies to extra-large and 'junior' sizes. Not all manufacturers use the same sizing categories (although 'mini', 'midi', 'maxi', 'maxi plus' and 'junior' are the most common) but will label the nappies with the weight range they are designed for, so it is not hard to tell which size you should be buying. The larger the size, the fewer nappies there (usually) are in the packet.

Some manufacturers produce both standard and luxury, or premium, versions of their nappies. Both will be very absorbent but the more expensive 'premium' range will have extras, such as a softer, cotton feel and an elasticated waistband.

How to choose

You may well experiment with two or three brands before you settle on a favourite, or you may stick with the first brand you buy. Either way, there are certain considerations you should be aware of.

Fit:

- a good disposable nappy should fit well with no gaps; be easy and quick to fasten, open and refasten; and should stay closed without the fastener losing its grip or tearing the nappy
- choose the smallest nappy your baby can comfortably wear – a size even slightly too big can be prone to leaks – but make sure you move up to the next size when it starts to seem a bit tight

Absorbency:

- don't go straight for a nappy that is advertised as being super-absorbent. Unless you buy a very basic and cheap brand, in which case inferior absorbency will probably be an issue, most nappies on the market should be able to cope successfully with your baby's output as long as you change the nappy regularly. Try out a standard supermarket own-brand nappy or a non-premium type of one of the big brands – you will probably be satisfied with the absorbency. You can save money by buying a cheaper brand of nappy for daytime use and a super-absorbent one for night-time when your baby will be wearing a nappy for a longer period of time.

Cost:

- buy the largest packs to reduce costs but be wary of bulk-buying too much in one size (especially newborn-size) as your baby may outgrow them sooner than you expect
- take advantage of special offers if you don't have a strong loyalty to one particular brand. Such is the competition between nappy manufacturers that offers such as '15 per cent extra free' or 'buy one get the second half price' are always to be found
- supermarkets and shops selling a range of nappy brands often make it easier for you to compare prices between brands by displaying the price per nappy alongside the pack price.

> "Nappies are really confusing. Manufacturers do different-size nappies, different-size boxes, different-size add-ons and different-size discounts – but they are all ultimately the same price. I work out the price per nappy with the calculator function on my mobile."
>
> Naomi, mother of Holly, 12 months

Nappy wars

The disposable nappy market is extremely competitive. The main manufacturers seem to be constantly re-inventing their products, and innovation after innovation appears on the nappy shelves. In order to get one step ahead of their competitors, manufacturers continually proclaim new developments in comfort, fit and absorbency – even the ability of a type of nappy to deal more efficiently with a particular sort of poo. At the time of writing, the trend is for 'stretchy' nappy materials, which are supposed to let your baby move around more freely. There also tend to be slight differences in the design of the nappy depending on the age of the baby they are intended for. Huggies, for example, re-launched its range with new, age-specific features: its 'Beginnings' range for new babies has an extra-soft lining for delicate new skin; 'Freedom' nappies for four-months-and-over babies, who are just starting to move and explore, have a 'control zone' for wetness; and 'Adventurers', for mobile babies of 12-months-plus, have an extra-slim fit and a 'double' leak guard on the legs.

The more gimmicky features developed by nappy manufacturers are quietly dropped after a while – for example, 'boy' and 'girl' nappies, which were supposed to offer extra protection in key areas according to gender, were the big thing in the nappy world in the late nineties but are now nowhere to be seen. However, some features may well help to keep your baby dry and more comfortable or make things easier for you when you are changing the nappy. Extras such as stretchy sides, a 'breathable' cotton-feel outer layer, Velcro fasteners (as opposed to reusable sticky tape) that won't lose their sticking power if you get nappy cream or talc on them (and won't stick to the skin) and effective waist- and leg-leak barriers have their appeal. You will pay a bit extra, of course, but you may decide that such features are worth having.

One innovation that may be worth a try is Pampers Total Care nappies for newborns and young babies. Pampers claims they 'absorb more soft, messy poo': a perforated top sheet is designed to let more poo through, which is then trapped inside and kept away from the baby's skin.

Washable nappies

Washable nappies have undergone a transformation in recent years. Traditional terry nappies, with their accompanying folding techniques and safety pins (and associated jokes about struggling, hapless dads), although still available, are used far less these days. There is nothing wrong with terry nappies – they are the cheapest nappies (around £20 for a pack of 12), wash well and dry quickly, and one size fits all – but more modern materials, fashions and lifestyles have changed the way that washable nappies are designed. These days, a baby in a washable nappy is likely to be wearing a soft, cotton, fitted nappy and cover with Velcro or popper fastenings and elasticated waist and legs. The nappies can look very much like disposables and can be put on and taken off just as easily; the only difference being that you wash them rather than throw them away.

How to choose

If you are new to the concept of fitted, washable nappies, the wide range of brands and types available can be confusing. You can get catalogues from specialist nappy companies which include everything from organic knitted tie-on nappies to towelling booster pads for extra absorbency. The basic choice, however, is between two-piece and one-piece nappies. Two-piece nappies consist of the nappy itself – which is usually made from cotton terry towelling or flannel, often with an element of polyester – and a separate outer wrap, which tends to be made from polyester with a waterproof layer. The nappies are shaped to fit and no folding is required, although you can also buy 'prefolds', which are flat nappies partly sewn into shape to make folding easier. These are held in place with safety pins or special plastic 'grippers'. The outer wrap and usually the nappy itself do up with either poppers or Velcro. The wrap gives extra security from leaks and keeps everything in its place. Although the nappies need to be washed after each use, the wraps don't, unless they have been soiled. One-piece nappies are similar to two-piece ones, but have an integral waterproof outer layer. They are quicker to put on and take off but they can be more difficult to keep clean and take longer to dry.

In addition to the one-piece or two-piece nappies, you can buy extra liners for times when additional absorbency is needed – night-time or travelling, for instance. Washable or disposable (and biodegradable) liners are available. Many people use liners on a daily basis – they can make nappy changes simpler because you can dispose of the liner and flush the solids away and keep the nappy itself going.

Looking after washable nappies

- Although they can be tumble-dried, if you are buying washable nappies for environmental reasons (see below), be aware that air-drying is more environmentally friendly. However, nappies can take 8–12 hours to dry, depending on the type, so you need to make sure you have the space and the spares to allow for this.
- Soaking prior to washing is recommended, so be prepared to live with nappy buckets full of soiled nappies.

Where to buy washable nappies

If you are going to be using washable nappies, it is recommended that you buy 20–30 nappies and four wraps. Washables are widely available these days and nursery stores such as Mothercare★ do sell them, but you are likely to find a much larger selection and more information from one of the many specialist mail-order nappy firms, such as Little Green Earthlets★ or the online cloth nappy catalogue, Twinkle Twinkle★, or direct from washable nappy manufacturers such as Bambino Mio★ and Cotton Bottoms★. UK Nappy Line★ can give you details of nappy suppliers, washing services and local 'nappy networks'. Take advantage of trial packs offered by manufacturers if you are not sure of which brand to buy – rather than make the expensive mistake of buying a bulk-load of nappies you are not happy with. If you want advice from other parents on reusable nappies, look at the cloth nappies chat forum on **www.ukparents.co.uk**, a parenting website. The site also operates a buy-and-sell forum for washable nappies.

> ❝ Josiah's nappies can come out of the washing machine looking quite stained but if I put them on the line in the sunshine, the stains disappear after an hour or so – it's something to do with a chemical reaction between the content of the stain and the sunlight. ❞
>
> Nicky, mother of Josiah, 7 months

> ❝ Seku is on a set of nappies that have been used by two other babies in the past and the absorbency seems fine. ❞
>
> Gillian, mother of Seku, 6 months

Nappy services
If you opt for washable nappies, you can avoid the extra washing by using a nappy service. As well as making things easier for you, the economies of scale involved in using a nappy washing service instead of washing nappies at home makes this the best option available in terms of environmental impact (see box on page 36). There are companies offering a nappy washing service throughout the UK, although they tend to be concentrated in urban areas. The company will pick up soiled nappies from your house and deliver freshly laundered ones. The nappies belong to the company and it will supply a deodorised nappy pail – you don't normally need to buy anything apart from the outer wraps. You will have the convenience of not having to worry about always maintaining a clean supply of nappies and not having to go to the shops to buy disposables. The main disadvantage is that using a nappy washing service works out a lot more expensive than home-washing nappies. Contact the National Association of Nappy Services (NANS)★ to find out if there are services in your area. If there is more than one service operating in your area, check what each is offering – some may have special introductory offers or there may be overall differences in price.

Nappy manufacturer Cotton Bottoms★ operates its own laundry scheme in some areas, mainly in southern England. The service costs around £12 per week. And as part of anti-waste policies, a handful of local councils also offer you a cash incentive of £30 or so if you sign up with a nappy laundry service. Check the Cotton Bottoms website to see if your local council runs one of these schemes.

Disposable versus washable nappies
Disposables are undoubtedly more convenient as you just throw them away after use – hence their huge popularity. They don't contribute towards your washing and are slim and light, so you can easily carry several around with you when you are out and about. A major disadvantage, however, is their cost. During the first few months you can expect to be changing a nappy about six times a day. A packet of newborn nappies from one of the main manufacturers works out at about 13p per nappy. So from the start you will be spending at least £5.50 a week, or £23 a month, on nappies.

Nappies and the environment

Disposable nappies have a significant environmental impact. Apart from the energy and materials used in their production, environmental organisations express concern that the widespread use of disposables is producing vast quantities of waste that could take hundreds of years to decompose. Disposables are used by 96 per cent of households with babies under one year of age, and it is estimated that one baby will get through around 5,000 nappies before he or she is toilet trained. Consequently, approximately eight million nappies enter the waste stream every day in the UK, and the vast majority of this ends up in landfill sites where parts of each nappy will take 200 years or more to decompose. Nappies make up at least 4 per cent of all household waste. The disposal of nappies is estimated to cost local authorities around £40 million a year – so local authorities, as well as environmental pressure groups, have an incentive to see this waste reduced.

Disposable nappies undeniably cause more waste than washable nappies, but washable nappies have their own environmental impact, albeit in different ways. Washing nappies at home means you use extra energy and water to keep them clean – resources you don't need to use with disposables. If you wash at high temperatures and use a tumble-drier this increases further the energy used. Manufacturers of disposables highlight facts such as this to defend the comparative environmental impact of disposables.

Both environmental organisations and disposable nappy manufacturers have produced their own studies, but the independent consensus is that there is, as yet, no clear answer as to which type of nappy is most environmentally friendly overall. However, because much of the environmental impact of washable nappies occurs during their use, parents can be proactive in minimising this. Using an economical wash cycle and line- or air-drying rather than tumble-drying is the environmentally friendlier route. Making sure the nappies get passed on to other babies is also a resource-saving way of using them. Using a nappy laundry service, however, is the greenest option for parents with a service in their area.

The environmental impact of disposables is another issue. Millions of disposable nappies are poured into landfill sites every week – eight million every day. Some parents choose not to use disposables because they don't like the idea of adding to this pile.

Washables work out cheaper than disposables, especially if you use traditional terry nappies rather than the more modern, fitted-style washable nappies (see pages 32 and 33). If you choose washable nappies you will be paying more at the outset – a 'set' of 20 fitted nappies can easily set you back £150 – but in the long run costs will be lower, especially if you use the nappies again for subsequent children. Washables don't create waste, but have their own environmental impact. In many ways, the jury is still out on whether washables have a clear environmental advantage over disposables (see box on previous page).

Because washable nappies can be less absorbent than disposables (some people find that they need to change their baby more often with washables), babies who use washable nappies are more likely to be toilet trained earlier, because they are more aware of the relationship between weeing and an uncomfortable nappy. Modern disposables are so absorbent that the child may not feel any wetness at all.

The main disadvantage with washables, of course, is that you have to soak and wash them. Some parents will use both washables and disposables so that they gain some of the advantages of both – perhaps using disposables when going out for the day or on holiday, and washables at other times.

Alternative disposables

In recognition that many environmentally concerned parents still have a strong desire for the convenience of disposables, a handful of small manufacturers have come up with disposable nappies which they claim have less impact on the environment than standard disposables. At the time of writing, two of the brands you are most likely to come across are 'Nature Boy and Girl' and 'Tushies'. The maker of Nature Boy and Girl – a Swedish nappy brand now available in UK supermarkets including Sainsbury's, for example – say its nappies contain 70 per cent renewable and biodegradable materials compared with 30–40 per cent in conventional nappies. The maker of Tushies nappies, which are available mainly in health-food-type shops, or direct from Beaming Baby★ or Green Baby★, stresses the fact that, unlike other disposable nappies, they don't use any chemical gel for absorbency, using highly absorbent cotton-blend padding instead. Of course, using these nappies still results in waste, but they may be worth a try if you want to continue using disposables but are keen to lessen the resulting environmental impact.

Nappy accessories
Some accessories will be more useful to you than others.

Baby wipes
You will be buying these for as long as your baby is using nappies. Wipes are basically soft cloth or paper rectangles impregnated with a moist cleansing formula. When your baby is newborn, cotton wool and warm water will usually be adequate for keeping his or her bottom clean, but you will be looking for something more efficient before long. Wipes normally come in oblong plastic packets with feed-through lids so you can pull the wipes out with one hand; for a small extra cost you can buy these packets in a plastic storage container, also with a feed-through lid. Wipes also come in drums, but these wipes tend to be thinner and smaller than those in packets so do not have quite the 'heavy duty' capacity you often need for cleaning up. They can also be more difficult to get at with one hand. You can buy standard, thick or extra-thick wipes: all will do the job well enough, although the thicker sort are more robust. Extra features that may appeal include 'built-in' baby lotion, extra-soft material or fragrance-free cleanser. There are significant price differences between supermarket own-brands and big-brand names such as Johnson & Johnson. Try the own-brands first – some people don't like them but you could find that they suit your needs perfectly well.

If you really want to pamper your baby, you can buy a Wipes Warmer (contact manufacturer Prince Lionheart★ for stockists) which keeps your wipes at a constantly warm temperature and supposedly more comfortable for your baby's bottom. However, it goes without saying that this is another product firmly at the 'unnecessary' end of the market.

Nappies and nappy rash

There is evidence to suggest that modern, highly absorbent disposable nappies can help prevent nappy rash because urine is very efficiently absorbed by the nappy, thus keeping the skin dry. If you use washable nappies you need to make sure they are properly cleaned and rinsed, as traces of ammonia or detergent may be left behind and these can trigger nappy rash. Using a nappy sanitiser such as Napisan or Bambino Mio's 'Nappy Fresh' when you soak the nappies should help reduce the likelihood of this. As an alternative to ordinary sanitising treatments, you can add to the nappy bucket 5 drops of tea tree oil (a natural antiseptic and disinfectant), or 1 tablespoon of sodium bicarbonate or 2–3 tablespoons of white distilled vinegar. Whatever type of nappy you use and however you look after your baby's bottom, a key way to help prevent nappy rash is to change the nappy regularly.

Nappy sacks

These are highly perfumed mini-plastic bags that you buy on a roll and which are designed to enable you to dispose of your nappies hygienically. You take the nappy off your baby, put it in the bag and then in the bin or somewhere else in preparation for disposal. The bags are effective at masking the smell of a dirty nappy but they are not a necessity. If you want to put the nappy in something before you throw it away, a standard plastic grocery bag tied up at the handles will do just as well – it won't have the same 'deodorising' effect, but some parents find the overpowering aroma of nappy sacks almost as bad as the nappy itself.

Nappy 'bins' and mesh bags

If you use disposable nappies and really don't like the idea of having soiled nappies in a normal bin in the house before they get thrown out, you can buy special nappy disposal 'units'. The nappy is placed in the unit and is automatically sealed into a plastic sleeve. You end up with a long string of sealed nappy parcels which you throw away when the unit is full. These units are widely available – Babies 'R' Us★, for example, sells the well-known Sangenic Disposable Nappy Wrapper for £29.99. It seals up to 180 nappies before you need to use a refill (the refill part is a round plastic 'cassette' full of nappy 'film', and you can buy these for around £3.50).

If you use reusable nappies you will need to have a nappy bucket for soaking soiled nappies. It should have a lid, an easy-to-use handle for when you need to empty the contents, and preferably a pouring lip. You can buy nappy buckets from nursery stores or specialist reusable nappy mail-order companies (see page 34). A nappy mesh bag can be a useful addition to a nappy bucket. The bag lines the bucket and keeps the soiled nappies together when you transfer them to the machine – you put the opened bag straight in the machine with the nappies inside. Little Green Earthlets★ sells nappy meshes for £3.95 each.

Changing mats

You can change your baby on a towel, but a changing mat is a relatively inexpensive item that can make changing your baby's nappy a bit easier. For one thing, it has a waterproof, wipe-clean plastic covering so that all those inevitable 'little accidents' can be easily cleaned up. Avoid changing mats with a towelling rather than a plastic covering – they may be more comfortable on your baby's bottom but you will probably end up washing the cover more often than you would wish (if you are really anxious about that cold bottom, you can put a normal towel on top of a standard changing mat anyway). Changing mats are padded so your baby won't feel the hard floor and they have slightly raised sides so that when your baby starts to squirm around it is more difficult for him or her to wriggle off the mat. Expect to pay about £7–8 for a standard changing mat available from any nursery store. This is all you really need, although there are mats at the 'luxury' end of the market: for example, Urchin★ sells a contoured mat, for £14.95, which is designed so your baby lies in a dip rather than on a flat surface so he or she is more inclined to stay in one place. Another type of changing mat is the Rabbitts★ Mat, costing £24.95, which incorporates a shoulder-and-waist harness so you have both hands free when trying to change the nappy of a struggling baby.

If you have bought or are planning to buy a changing bag (see pages 164 and 165), it will probably include a 'travel' changing mat. These can be useful when you are out and about. Nappy manufacturers on the lookout for gaps in a crowded market have recently come up with disposable changing mats. There is no

Safety watch

The floor is the safest place to change your baby. Even if you have the mat on a changing table you should not leave your baby's side in case he or she wriggles off (for more on changing tables or units, see pages 86–90). If you change your baby on the floor, you can be a bit more relaxed.

point in getting one of these if you already have a portable changing mat, and even if you don't they are one more item in the long list of baby products you can easily do without.

Dummies

These simple pieces of plastic can provoke all sorts of emotions. Some parents hate the idea of their child having a dummy – often for aesthetic reasons as much as anything – and would prefer that a thumb or finger is sucked. Others come to regard the dummy as their saviour and a piece of equipment they can't bear to think of being without (woe betide the parent who forgets the favourite dummy on a long car journey or day trip). Some of the parents in the latter category will have originally been in the former, but will have succumbed to the undeniably attractive temptation of an instant soother that doesn't involve a nipple!

Babies themselves often have strong preferences. Some babies seem to have a clear need for 'non-nutritive' sucking. The comfort provided by the dummy can become addictive – you can be sure that if social embarrassment and parental pressure to give up had not taken effect by the post-toddler stage, some children would happily go to school with a dummy in their bag. Other babies simply don't like dummies, no matter how keen their parents are for them to have one. You will soon know if your baby is one of these.

Although it is easier said than done, you should aim to restrict the use of a dummy as much as possible, whatever type you use. Confining it to sleep times is a good principle, but prepare yourself for the fact that it will be very tempting to break this rule whenever you are faced with a grouchy baby. In the longer term, it is worth bearing in mind there is some evidence to show that babies who get very reliant on their dummy may be slower to develop language skills than other children.

Types of dummy

As with teats for bottles (see pages 102–3), dummy teats are made from either latex or silicone mounted on a plastic shield. Silicone teats are preferable from a parent's point of view. They are easier to keep clean and are more hard-wearing. They also don't have the rubbery smell of latex, which you may notice if your baby is an ardent sucker of a latex dummy. On the other hand, babies themselves often prefer latex because it is more flexible and softer to suck. If you plan to give your baby a dummy, try a silicone teat first and move on to rubber if this is not acceptable.

The shape of the teat may also be an issue. You can buy dummies with either an orthodontic teat or a traditional bell-shaped teat. If you are not confident that you will be able to limit your baby's dummy use to the first few months (before he or she develops a set of teeth), try an orthodontic teat first. Although a dummy won't cause problems to future permanent teeth, constant and sustained sucking could disturb the alignment of baby teeth and an orthodontic teat is designed to cause the least disturbance. If your baby prefers a bell shape to an orthodontic shape, however, it is nothing to panic about. Thumb-sucking is more of an issue when it comes to teeth because you can't take your baby's thumb away.

Points to consider

- Buy two or more at a time. Dummies get lost easily so it is always worth having a few spares.
- Some brands come in plastic containers. These are handy for keeping your dummies clean.
- You can buy dummy chains, with clips that attach to your baby's clothing at one end and to the dummy at the other end – these are useful if your baby is constantly dropping his or her dummy.
- Check the condition of dummies regularly and throw away any that seem damaged or worn.
- Sterilise young babies' dummies regularly (see pages 103–7 for information on sterilising).

> ### Safety watch
>
> *Never hang a dummy round your baby's neck on a ribbon (as has been a practice in the past) as this is a strangulation hazard.*

"Don't buy an obscure make of dummy. Make sure from the start it's a type, brand and even colour combination that is widely available and you can get from any chain chemist or supermarket. Cal will only have a pale blue dummy that only seems to be sold in small independent grocers' shops. I've had to drive miles going in and out of a variety of these shops trying to find one that sells the right sort. It's a good incentive to get him to give up though!**"**

Chris, father of Cal, age 2

Bouncy cradles

A bouncy cradle, or baby chair, is a relatively inexpensive piece of equipment that you can get a lot of use out of during the first few months (you should stop using it when your baby can sit). It provides a safe place for parking a wide-awake baby when you have both hands busy with other tasks. Sessions in the chair can give your baby a change of scene and, because seated and harnessed in at a slant, he or she can watch you as you do whatever you are doing. Some chairs are more padded than others and have a recline position so you can use them as an extra dozing place (although they are not really suitable for lengthy sessions because they do not provide the same support as a cot or a pram). Others have a simpler design. All can also be used as a convenient feeding chair when your baby is being weaned but is still too young for the highchair.

Types of bouncy cradle

Although there are variations within each category, there are three main types of bouncy cradle. Automated baby swings, also covered here, are a further option.

Wire-framed cradles

This is the simplest style. Fabric is stretched around a wire frame, which is at a reclining angle and curves round to a flat base. You can gently bounce the cradle by jigging the frame.

Pros:

✔ the least expensive type, they normally cost around £15–20

✔ basic style but perfectly adequate for its purpose

✔ light and easy to move around the house.

Cons:

✘ no recline position and little or no padding, so may be less comfortable for your baby if he or she wants to snooze

✘ non-folding so difficult to put out of sight.

Padded, tubular-framed cradles

More luxurious than the wire-framed models, these usually have adjustable lie-back positions as well as extra padding. They are fairly sturdy and have a more rounded appearance than the wire-framed type. Some models have carrying handles and you can often adjust the cradle to have either a fixed or rocking base.

Pros:

✔ versatile because of features such as the adjustable lie-back

✔ rounded sides and more cradle-like shape, so may help your baby feel more secure

✔ fold-flat models available.

Cons:

✘ more expensive than the wire-framed version: expect to pay £25–55, depending on the model

✘ you may not use the extra features for which you are paying more.

Automated cradles

These are really a cross between a bouncy cradle and an automated baby swing (see opposite). You can normally opt to have them in the standard bouncy chair mode or in the vibrating mode, which is meant to gently simulate the vibrations of a car engine. The vibrations are battery-powered and you can adjust the speed.

Pros:

✔ vibrating motion can be an effective soother – if you have to take the car out to get your baby to sleep, an automated cradle could be a convenient alternative

✔ not necessarily more expensive than the non-automated types (Mothercare's★ cheapest costs £37).

Cons:

✘ vibrating motion may well be an unnecessary extra – most babies will be perfectly happy with the standard manual bounce and some may even dislike the vibrations

✘ extra noise caused by the vibrations may be irritating.

Automated baby swings

These comprise a padded chair or swing on a rigid metal or plastic frame. They are battery-operated; turn them on and your baby swings gently without your having to lift a finger. Swings generally have a two-speed rocking mechanism, although you can buy ones that have up to ten speeds. They require 4 'D' batteries, which provide about 200 hours of swinging. Some come with extras such as a play tray with toys and music that plays while the swing is in motion. Baby swings are usually suitable for babies from birth to 11kg (about ten months) and are widely available in nursery stores. Expect to pay £60–110.

Pros:

✔ can soothe many babies to sleep (they also have a reputation for calming colicky babies)

✔ provides an extra place for you to 'park' your baby and gives him or her a bit of variety too.

Cons:

✘ quite expensive for an item that will only be in use for a few months (nine to ten at the most) and which your baby may not even like

✘ takes up a lot of space in the living room.

Points to consider before you buy

- If your baby seems happy using the infant car seat (see pages 136–46) as an indoor seat, especially if it is a seat with a rocking motion, a bouncy cradle may well be a superfluous piece of equipment.
- Some models have removable, washable seat covers (as opposed to sponge-clean) – these are much more practical if you are likely to use the cradle as a feeding chair at some time.
- Bouncy cradles can take up space – look for a fold-flat model if you mind the idea of it as a semi-permanent fixture.
- Some bouncy cradles come with toy bars, which can provide added entertainment value for your baby; alternatively, you can simply position a baby gym over the chair.
- A head-support cushion is included with many models – this can be useful for very young babies.
- Padding is not a crucial feature – cradles without padding still provide adequate support.
- Because you will only be using the cradle for a few months it may be worth bypassing the more expensive end of the market.

Safety watch

Never place a bouncy cradle on a raised surface such as a table-top. One unexpected lurch forward from your baby could send him or her flying or skidding off and could cause serious injury. For the same reason, never place a cradle outside next to a paddling pool or garden pond. Babies have drowned when their parents' attention has been diverted in this kind of situation.

Baby baths

During the early weeks, a baby bath enables you to bathe your baby without having to stoop over the main bath and allows you to do it in a room other than the bathroom. Bathing your baby in the living room next to a warm fire, or in your bedroom or the nursery, may be more convenient and cosier than in a chilly bathroom (remember towels around the bath for the inevitable splashes). However, you don't have to buy a baby bath. Many parents like to have a bath with their baby – the skin-to-skin contact this provides can be a pleasant experience for both baby and parent. Alternatively, you can bathe your baby in the kitchen sink lined with a towel or foam bath support (see below) for comfort. As long as the washing-up is cleared away and the surfaces are clean, the sink serves as a convenient, waist-height bathing platform. Newborn babies do not actually need to have a complete bath for a couple of weeks or so, anyway. Instead, you can opt to 'top and tail' them – you just need two small bowls of warm water and some cotton wool for washing the face/upper body and bottom separately. Or you can buy 'top and tail' bowls with two separate compartments in one bowl (Mothercare★ sells these for £3).

The lifespan of a baby bath may be fairly short – by the time your baby is a month or two old, a standard baby bath may well be too small and the splashes too large to make it of continued usefulness. But for the brief period before this, a baby bath can be a helpful, if non-essential, item to have. Other bath products (see below) are used in different ways and may have a longer lifespan. If you have a changing unit this may come with a baby bath, so you won't need to buy a separate one (for more on changing units, see pages 86–90).

Types of bath
A selection of types of bath and bath supports is available.

Standard baby baths
There is a choice of simple, oval-shaped baths or baths with a slightly angled shape for extra ease of handling and support. Whichever sort you go for, a slip-resistant textured base is an important feature (soapy babies are notoriously slippery). You should also check that the bath is sturdy and made of firm moulded plastic – cheap, thin plastic can bow with the weight of the water. A drainage hole and plug can be helpful for emptying the water, but are not essential. Easy-to-grip sides or handles are, however, because you may be moving the bath around when it is full of water. Expect to pay £8–15 for a standard baby bath from one of the leading nursery equipment chain stores.

Pros:

✔ versatile – you can use the bath in the main bath or anywhere else in the house (even outside in the garden on warm days).

Can be placed on a secure table or bed so you can bathe your baby at a comfortable height

✔ small babies may feel more secure in the compact shape of a baby bath as opposed to a normal bath.

Cons:

✘ takes up a fair amount of storage space for something with such a short lifespan.

Rest-on-rim baths

These are baby baths with either a very wide rim or supports at either end, designed so that you can rest them on the rim of the main bath. They should have a plug-hole so you can empty the water out easily into the main bath.

Pros:

✔ your baby is positioned at a convenient kneeling height so you don't have to bend right over the bath

✔ can also be used as a stand-alone bath.

Cons:

✘ more expensive than standard baths (expect to pay £18–20)

✘ same lifespan and storage restrictions as standard baths

✘ if your main bath is a non-standard shape or is particularly large or small, the rest-on-rim bath won't fit.

Bath supports

A variety of different products come into this category, but they all work in roughly the same way. Your baby is normally bathed in the main bath but lies on some sort of soft pad, wire-rimmed mesh fabric support or rigid plastic 'seat', so his or her body is not fully immersed but can still be easily washed. The baby's head is supported above the water line. Products range from simple foam supports (try Mothercare's★ Foam Support at £6) to floating polystyrene-filled bathing pads (£11.99 from JoJo Maman Bébé★) and contoured bath chairs (£17.99 from Blooming Marvellous★ and JoJo Maman Bébé).

Pros:

✔ comfortable for your baby, particularly the soft supports

✔ your hands are free to concentrate on washing and pulling silly faces

✔ your baby may feel happier not being fully immersed

✔ easy to store; light and compact enough for travel.

Cons:

✗ your baby may not have the freedom to wriggle and splash as in a normal bath, and you won't be able to swish him or her around in the same way

✗ foam supports in particular need to be taken out of the bath and squeeze-dried carefully to prevent mildew developing.

Bath rings

These are designed for babies who can sit unaided, so should only be used from around six months. They comprise a seat with an in-between legs support, surrounded by a waist-height ring of plastic. Suction pads on the bottom attach to the main bath. The idea is that your baby stays sitting upright while being washed and can also play without moving around too much or slipping. Some models have swivelling seats (for example, Mothercare★ sells one for £12), so your baby has a bit more freedom of movement.

Pros:

✔ keeps your baby in one place so you can wash him or her easily

✔ may help some babies feel more secure in the bath.

Cons:

✗ active babies who want to play in the bath may find their movements restricted

✗ some babies may struggle being put in the ring or it may be difficult to get them out

✗ there is a risk that bath rings may give parents a false sense of security and tempt them to pay less attention to their baby. For this reason, the Consumers Union in the United States even says that bath rings are best avoided. Babies should never be left unattended in a bath, no matter what bath device you are using.

Bucket baths

Shaped like a large bucket, these baths are apparently popular in continental Europe but are not yet widely available in the UK (JoJo Maman Bébé★ sells them for £12.99). They are designed so your baby is washed in a sitting or pre-natal foetal position rather than a lying position.

Pros:

✔ small babies may feel more secure being bathed in the foetal position
✔ uses less water and space than conventional baby baths
✔ easier shape to carry when full
✔ water stays warm for longer.

Cons:

✘ same limited lifespan as conventional baths – they are recommended for babies up to six months, but a chubby, lively pre-six-monther may well find the bath constricting
✘ limited space for playing with bath toys or for being swished around.

Other bath accessories

You don't need a lot of equipment at bathtime, but the following items can have their uses.

Non-slip bath mat

This is one of the few items of equipment you do genuinely need, once your baby starts sitting and pulling up without your support. Slippery babies and toddlers and a slippery bath will eventually result in an accident. A bath mat provides a safe, non-slip surface. There are lots of bath mats designed specifically for children with fun designs on them, even with built-in thermometers. You will pay extra for these features, of course, and a standard bath mat will do the job perfectly well. Unusual-shaped children's bath mats or bath appliqués (mini non-slip shapes often in the form of splashes or fishes) can even be less effective because they may not cover as much of the bottom of the bath. For extra reassurance, a full-length bath mat can work well, particularly if you are bathing more than one child – these mats are fairly widely available or you can buy one from JoJo Maman Bébé★ for £9.99.

Hooded baby towels

These hooded, cape-shaped towels, or 'cuddle robes', are a bit gimmicky. Babies look cute in them (they often have children's character motifs on the hood) and the hood may help keep them warm – but a soft fluffy towel can do the job just as well or better. They are widely available from nursery stores: expect to pay £10–12.

Tap cover

Although not an issue with younger babies, once babies start pulling themselves up and moving around independently in the bath, there is a risk they could slip or tumble and bang their head against the taps (particularly if you have another child in the bath too). Some toddlers also have a fascination with trying to turn on the hot tap. One option is to cover the taps with a wet towel or protect the handles with cut plastic drinks bottles. Alternatively, you can buy a tap cover designed specifically for this purpose – JoJo Maman Bébé★ sells an inflatable tap cover for £5.99.

Bath toy tidy

Plastic toys from all over the house will probably end up in the bath, and you will want to be able to tidy them and dry them quickly and easily. A bath toy tidy is a mesh bag which you attach with suction pads to the bathroom tiles above the bath. The mesh allows the water to drain away or air-dry easily, and the toys are always at hand to tip into the bath again. As your baby gets older, or you have more than one child in the bath, you may find that the bag isn't big enough to hold the range of toys that are required at bathtime, so you could end up with a collection perched around the bath edge or thrown into a box anyway. Bath toy tidies are widely available from nursery stores, price £3–6.

Bath thermometer

Running a warm bath for your baby shouldn't be a complicated procedure requiring extra technical equipment. You can easily test the heat of the bath with the time-honoured method of sticking your elbow or wrist in the water and trusting your instinct. For extra safety you should run the cold tap first followed by the hot. If you feel especially anxious, however, a bath thermometer (see page 196) should prove helpful.

Safety tip
If your hot water seems very hot, making it difficult to get the temperature of the bath right, turn down the thermostat.

Baby toiletries

The wealth of baby toiletry products available is staggering. From standard chain-store own-brand baby shampoos to relatively pricey washes and moisturisers – containing extracts of everything from milk proteins to lavender and chamomile oils – the baby-beauty market is big business. Of course, the fancier products appeal more to the personal tastes of parents rather than having any demonstrable benefit over cheaper alternatives (unless a skin condition such as eczema is involved, in which case a specific product may be recommended).

When it comes to the practicalities of washing your baby and looking after his or her skin, you really don't need much and it is usually a case of the simpler the better. Bear the following in mind.

- For most babies, a bottle of simple baby bath is all you will need. Shampooing isn't actually necessary until they are a few weeks old. You can buy baby baths that double-up as shampoos – and fewer bottles can mean an easier bathtime.
- Newborn babies don't actually need any bath products at all – warm water is sufficient.
- Talcum powder is, arguably, an unnecessary product whatever the baby's age – make sure you dry him or her properly and see whether this suffices before starting to use it.
- If your baby's skin seems dry, a touch of mild, unperfumed baby lotion or moisturiser may help, or you can put a couple of drops of olive oil in the bath. If the dryness seems to be irritating your baby, try an emollient such as Oilatum in the bath. This is more expensive than standard products but you may be able to get it free on prescription if you visit your GP.
- Don't bother with toiletry 'gift' or 'starter' packs where you get a selection of different toiletries – you're unlikely to find much use for more than one or two of the bottles in the pack.

> **❝** My midwife recommended cotton wool pads rather than balls for cleaning Lara's skin because they don't fray and disintegrate. I've tried them both and the pads do seem better – the only drawback is they are more expensive. **❞**
>
> Kerry, mother of Lara, 4 weeks

First bath tips

Follow these guidelines for bathing your baby in the first few months.

- *Make sure the room is warm.*
- *Gather together everything you need before you undress your baby.*
- *When you run the water into the bath, run the cold water first. Test the temperature with your elbow or wrist. The ideal temperature is 37°C – which is comfortably warm but not hot.*
- *Lower your baby into the bath with his or her head supported with your forearm and your other hand around his or her bottom.*
- *Keep bathtime short – young babies get cold easily.*
- *Pay special attention to folds in the skin, such as those around your baby's neck and legs, when you are drying.*

Baby monitors

Parents fall into two main camps when it comes to monitors: those who regard them as an indispensable piece of baby equipment and those who can't see any reason to have one.

The purpose of a baby monitor is to allow you to hear your baby crying when you are in another part of the house or in the garden. It can be a useful device to have if you are concerned that you won't hear your baby's cries. A few new parents, however, can become preoccupied with the supposed value of their monitor, keeping a close watch on it and listening out for every snuffle and grunt as confirmation that their baby is still breathing. But monitors are not safety devices and, although you can get devices that monitor breathing, healthy babies do not need to be monitored in this way. A monitor should be regarded as a device for parents' convenience.

As part of the baby-product buying bonanza that prospective parents often feel under pressure to take part in, monitors have achieved a degree of 'must-have' status. But if you can hear your baby crying when you are in the house or flat, you certainly don't need one. Keeping doors open is a cheaper way of ensuring you can hear your baby. There is also an argument that monitors can encourage parents to over-pamper: babies will often cry and fuss for a short time then settle themselves back to sleep, but if parents are rushing to soothe their baby at the merest whimper, this could contribute towards future sleeping problems (although some monitors can be set so that only the real cries are transmitted – a handy option once anxious parents become more relaxed).

That said, many parents do find monitors to be extremely handy. If you have a pet and need to keep bedroom doors firmly closed, for example, they keep your baby within earshot. Even if you find you don't need to use one on a daily basis, they can have valuable occasional uses – for example, if you are having friends round for a drink and a chat and you want to know above the din that your baby is settled, or if you need to do some work in the garden and you are out of earshot, a portable monitor (some must be plugged into a socket and are not portable) will let you keep tabs on your baby. If you are deaf or hard-of-hearing, a monitor – particularly one with a visual display (see below) – will have clear benefits.

Caution!

Bear in mind that what you say in your baby's room while the monitor is switched on could be picked up by your neighbours via their own monitors.

Before choosing a monitor you need to decide how useful it would be, taking into consideration the layout of your home and your normal everyday activities. You will probably have a better idea about this if you wait until after the birth before you buy.

Types of monitor
All monitors are made up of two units. You keep one unit with you or near you and the other next to the baby. The unit next to the baby

transmits to your unit, via radio waves (you will usually have a choice of two channels so you can switch if you are getting interference on one), any sounds he or she makes. The usual operating range is 100 metres. Most can be either mains or battery operated; some have rechargeable batteries. Some models need to be plugged into a socket and have no battery-power facility.

Mains-powered monitors

These can be plugged into a socket in any room but cannot be used with batteries. They are the simplest type of monitor.

Pros:
✔ the least expensive option (the Tomy★ Babylink model is £17 from Mothercare★)
✔ ideal for parents who won't be moving around the house much while the monitor is on, or if they are only likely to be using the monitor at night.

Cons:
✗ less versatile because you can't use batteries.

Portable, dual-powered monitors

These run on either the mains or batteries, so the parent unit can be carried around with you when on battery power – some come with a belt clip so you don't need to hold it. The more expensive models in this category have rechargeable batteries.

Pros:
✔ useful for parents who will be busying themselves about the house or garden while the baby is asleep
✔ rechargeable models are easy to recharge and save you worrying about batteries running out.

Cons:
✗ more expensive than mains-powered models (expect to pay £30–50 for the simpler models and up to £130 for the most sophisticated digital models; see page 57).
✗ you may find you don't use the portable facility enough to justify the extra expense

✗ if you regularly run a non-rechargeable model on batteries, you could find the extra cost of batteries a burden.

Extra features

The more you pay for your monitor, the more sophisticated the features are likely to be. Some of these have greater potential use than others. They include the following.

- **Visual light display** – this is one of the more useful extra features. It allows you to turn off the sound, and a sound-activated multi-light display panel shows whether or not your baby is crying. The louder your baby cries, the more lights are illuminated. If you don't want to hear your baby's every snuffle while you are sitting down to relax, a light display could be handy. It could also be useful in a situation when, for example, you have friends round or are having a meeting with someone at home and you don't want your baby's fussing to disturb things.
- **Nightlight on baby unit** – this gives the area around the unit a soft glow, which may be of comfort to your baby and can help you to see him or her better in a darkened room. If you have this feature on your monitor you are unlikely to want a separate nightlight too; however, depending on the intensity of the light, it may be too soft to be of particular use.
- **Volume warning** – some models will vibrate to warn you if you have the volume on your unit too low.
- **Temperature display** – a temperature sensor on the baby unit tells you the temperature of the room. If you are worried about controlling the temperature in your baby's room, however, you can buy a cheap nursery thermometer (for about £3) instead of choosing a monitor for this extra feature. Bear in mind, though, that your baby's temperature is not being monitored – an effective way of checking whether your baby is too hot or cold is by feeling his or her stomach.
- **Lullaby trigger** – a soothing lullaby is automatically activated if your baby stirs. The effectiveness of this will depend on the individual baby and has the potential to be more irritating than soothing.

- **Out-of-range alarm** – if you get preoccupied and, for example, wander to the end of the garden so you are out of range, an alarm sounds. This could be useful as a means of helping you assess how far down the garden you can go, but it is hard to see how it would be useful again once you have found this out (unless you are particularly absent-minded).

- **Multi-channel options** – two channels should be adequate for most people, but if you live in a busy, built-up area with lots of other parents with monitors in close proximity, creating the likelihood of regular interference, the option of more channels may be helpful.

- **Digital technology** – some models have microprocessors designed to ensure that the only nursery sounds you will be able to hear are those from your own nursery, not anyone else's. However, this doesn't stop the transmissions from your own monitor being picked up by somebody else.

- **Two-way talk-back** – you can use the parent's unit to talk to your child. This means you can make soothing noises to your baby if he or she starts to wake up and (probably of greater use) you can talk to an older child who has trouble settling down at bedtime.

- **Long range** – a small number of monitors transmit further than the standard 100 metres (one model transmits up to 400 metres). Although this may seem a useful feature in theory, in practice it is not such a good idea to be this far away from your baby.

Breathing and movement monitors

A small number of monitors are designed to check for breathing and movement as well as noise. A sensor pad is placed under the mattress to monitor these signs of life. Monitors like this are not considered by everyone to be a good idea. The Foundation for the Study of Infant Deaths (SIDS)* says that healthy babies don't need to be monitored in this way and that there is no evidence this kind of monitoring can prevent cot death. An alarm sounds if there is no movement detected for 15–20 seconds, but there are situations when a baby could stop breathing but still be moving: if he or she is choking, for example. If a baby does stop breathing and the alarm sounds, parents or carers would need to know resuscitation techniques (a video on this may be included with the monitor). There is also an argument that monitors like these can feed parents' insecurities about cot death and make putting a healthy baby to sleep an unnecessarily anxious time. Some models even have highly emotive names – for instance, the Angelcare monitor from Safety 1st, which has an unusual shape resembling an angel complete with halo. There is also the anxiety-increasing risk of false alarms – one major manufacturer withdrew its alarm from the market because of complaints from parents about false alarms. If you are worried about cot death, you should talk to your doctor or health visitor first rather than make a beeline for one of these monitors.

Video monitors

You can watch your baby's every move 'live' on your television or on a separate mini-screen on the parent unit. These monitors have a small camera that you position to view your baby. When they are linked to the TV screen you can normally set them to an automatic mode so, if you are watching television and your baby starts to cry, your TV viewing is interrupted so you can see your baby and judge whether you need to go and tend to him or her. The camera has a wide-angled lens and can transmit pictures in the dark. Pictures are in black and white or colour, depending on the model. At £100-200, such monitors are most definitely at the luxury end of the market. If you do buy one, they have the potential to be more useful later on when you may need to keep an eye on a mischievous toddler or older child.

Baby crying analyser

A fairly recent product on the market is the WhyCry monitor. This differs from other monitors in that it 'analyses' your baby's cries, the idea being that you have a better idea of what the cries mean (hungry, sleepy, in pain, and so on) and can deal with the situation accordingly. You use a symptoms chart along with the monitor to help you analyse the cry. Arguably, this monitor may be an added aid during the early weeks when you are lacking confidence, but you don't need one; parents tend to learn what their baby's cries mean naturally just by being attentive.

Anti-cot-death products

Although cot death is rare, most parents worry about it to some degree when they have a new baby. Manufacturers have tapped into such parental anxieties, and in recent years a range of anti-cot-death products have come on to the market. These range from sleeping-position aids, which are designed to ensure your baby sleeps in the recommended position (see pages 85 and 86) to breathing monitors (see page 57 and 58). Baby sleeping bags, although not designed as an anti-cot-death aid, have also had publicity for their anti-cot-death qualities (namely that your baby's head can't get covered by bedding). However, the bottom line is that you don't need to buy specialist products to guard against cot death unless recommended to do so by your doctor or hospital because your baby is viewed as being at particular risk. It's true that some products can help put your mind at rest if you are a particularly anxious new parent, but you shouldn't view them as a necessity for the safety of your baby. Bear in mind too that there are retailers who make particularly over-the-top claims for the products they sell – one retailer of baby mattress covers advertises them as providing '100 per cent successful prevention of cot death'.

The Foundation for the Study of Infant Deaths (SIDS)★ gives very clear advice on putting your baby to sleep and on the risk factors known to be linked to cot death (see Chapter 3). If you follow this advice you'll be taking all the precautions with your baby's sleeping environment that you need to take – without the need to spend extra money on unnecessary and often expensive products.

Websites

Asda	www.asda.co.uk
Babies 'R' Us	www.babiesrus.co.uk
Baby Planet	www.baby-planet.co.uk
Bambino Mio	www.bambino.co.uk
Beaming Baby	www.beamingbaby.com
Blooming Marvellous	www.bloomingmarvellous.co.uk
Charlie Crow	www.charliecrow.com
Cotton Bottoms	www.cottonbottoms.co.uk
Foundation for the Study of Infant Deaths	www.sids.org.uk/fsid
The Great Little Trading Company	www.gltc.co.uk
Green Baby	www.greenbabyco.com
JoJo Maman Bébé	www.jojomamanbebe.co.uk
Little Green Earthlets	www.earthlets.co.uk
Marks and Spencer	www.marksandspencer.co.uk
Mini Boden	www.boden.co.uk
Mischief Kids	www.mischiefkids.co.uk
Mothercare	www.mothercare.co.uk
National Association of Nappy Services	www.changeanappy.co.uk
Prince Lionheart	www.princelionheart.co.uk
Rabbitts	www.rabbitts.com
Starchild	www.starchildshoes.com
Sunday Best	www.sundaybestchristening.com
Tomy	www.tomy.co.uk
Twinkle Twinkle	www.twinkleontheweb.co.uk
UK Nappy Line	www.nappyline.org.uk
UKparents	www.ukparents.co.uk
Urchin	www.urchin.co.uk
Woolworths	www.woolworths.co.uk

First essentials checklist

Item	Notes
Sleeping place & bedding (Ch 3)	
Clothing	
Scratch mittens	
Shawl/blanket	
Nappies	
Baby wipes/cotton wool	
Nappy sacks	
Nappy bin	
Mesh bags	
Changing mat/unit	
Bottles, formula, steriliser (Ch 4)	
Bibs/muslin cloths (Ch 4)	
Breast pads/feeding bra/ pump (Ch 4)	
Dummies	
Car seat (Ch 5)	
Pushchair/pram/carrier (Ch 6)	
Bouncy cradle	
Baby bath	
Non-slip bath mat	
Other bath accessories	
Bath thermometer (Ch 7)	
Toiletries	
Baby monitor	
Other	

Chapter 3

Furnishing the nursery

One of the most pleasurable aspects of preparing for a baby can be getting the nursery ready. No matter that your baby may not be sleeping there for a few months to come (the recommendation from the Foundation for the Study of Infant Deaths (SIDS)* is that babies sleep in your room until they are six months old) – there is still something satisfying in giving the room a lick of paint, choosing new curtains or simply putting up some shelves to cope with the bundles of cuddly toys that will shortly be amassing.

You are likely to be using the nursery for a whole range of baby-focused activities, from nappy changing to clothes storage, before your baby moves into the room. It will help you in the post-birth weeks if you can get the basic decorating and sorting done before the baby is born. However, it is sensible to wait before buying lots of equipment. You will develop a sense of the kinds of things you could usefully buy and those you can do without, and you may, for example, discover that you are happy with changing nappies on the floor, so that pricey changing unit you had your eye on would have been an unnecessary luxury.

Bear in mind too that you need to be thinking of your own comforts as well as those of your baby. It is worth devoting some of your energy to arranging matters such as a comfortable chair for feeding (low arm-rests are best; see page 92 for more about nursing chairs) – you could have this in the nursery or your bedroom for night-time feeds if you are not comfortable feeding in bed.

A place to sleep

Cots

A cot is one of the few items you really do need for your baby, although even so you don't have to rush into buying one ready for your newborn. A Moses basket, carry cot or crib (see pages 68–71) may be more practical when your baby is tiny – they all have plus points that can make the early days easier for you. Cots are equally fine for new babies. It is all a matter of personal preference.

Choosing a cot

There are so many different styles of cots around that many parents find the process of buying a cot a bit confusing. After all, along with a pushchair or pram, it is probably the most significant purchase you will make for your baby, so you want to get it right first time. The main differences, however, are fairly straightforward. Bear in mind that cots are rarely sold with an inclusive mattress, so you'll need to buy one separately.

Which size?

Cots vary in size. Cots designed to fit 'standard-sized' mattresses are a few centimetres narrower than cots designed for 'continental-sized' mattresses, although they are often a similar length. Cots will vary in size within these 'standard' and 'continental' categories too. Cot beds, which are cots that convert into child-size beds, will be larger still and need special cot-bed-sized mattresses. Look at a few cots before you buy to see if a larger size would be better for you – measurements should be clearly displayed on the cot label too. The obvious advantage of a larger cot is that your baby will have more room – this may be more significant later on if the cot is used as a place to relax in the mornings: to look at picture books or play with toys. If your baby and you are happy to continue to use a cot until he or she is well into the toddling years, a larger cot may also be more practical. However, small cots are perfectly adequate for a growing baby and they may be a better choice if space in your home is cramped. They also tend to be cheaper.

Fixed- or drop-sides?

Most cots available have drop-sides. One side of the cot will have a mechanism that is designed to let you lower the side so you can lift your baby in and out with ease, particularly when you have the base positioned at the lowest level (see below). Some cots have drop-mechanisms on both sides, so as long as the cot is not next to a wall you can choose which side to use.

How useful a drop-side is depends largely on the efficiency of the mechanism. Some designs work a lot more smoothly than others. 'Nudge and lift' mechanisms, whereby you push the side of the cot into a position where it can be lowered, can be useful because you can operate them with one hand. Many parents find it takes a while to master this, however. Other cots will have a trigger mechanism, a foot pedal or a couple of catches which you undo.

Drop-sides can certainly be useful early on, but aim to try out a few different types in the shops before you buy, and choose the one that seems easiest for you to use. Many parents (especially the taller ones) find the whole process over-fiddly and prefer to lift their baby in and out without dropping the cot side.

Solid ends or rails all round?

Some parents prefer a cot with rails all the way around because it's easier to see your baby if you just want to peek into the room (depending on where the cot is positioned, of course). The cot may also seem more open and airy to your baby. Solid ends, however, do give a cot a sturdier, solid look and you may prefer the more enclosed feel.

Height-adjustable base

The base height of most cots can be adjusted as your baby grows. A height-adjustable feature is especially useful if you are using a cot as opposed to a crib or Moses basket from birth. It means you can have the cot base on its highest level for the first few months, so you can lift your baby in and out of it easily. Then, when your baby starts to move around more and pull him- or herself up, you can reposition the base at the lower level so that he or she stays secure in the cot. Cots tend to have either a two- or three-position base, although a few have more. Two positions are usually fine for most people's needs.

Teething rail

You won't know in the early days if your baby is going to be a cot-gnawer. However, chomping on the edge of a cot is a habit many babies do seem to relish. The teeth-marks will certainly make your cot look less than new within a few months, but they won't make it unusable. A teething rail is a protective covering lining the side-edges of the cot. Choose a cot with one of these if you would rather avoid the risk of damage. (Note that the risk is only to the cot, not to your baby!)

Casters

Some cots have casters, which can be a useful feature for making moving the cot from your room to the baby's room, or to a different position in the nursery, as smooth as possible. It also makes for easier cleaning under and around the cot.

Other types of cots

You don't have to buy a traditional cot. Other styles and designs are widely available, which, as well as looking a bit different, may have features that suit your needs better.

Cot beds

A cot bed is a cot with removable sides and end panel so that it can be converted into a toddler-sized bed when needed. These are increasingly popular and seem a logical way of lengthening the life of a cot as well as helping to make the move from a cot to a bed as smooth as possible for your child. Cot beds are larger than cots but are not necessarily much more expensive – Mothercare*, for example, sells a simply designed cot bed for £140. You will need to buy a cot-bed-sized mattress rather than one designed for a cot.

Cot beds can be a practical option and suit many parents and children very well. However, you do need to think carefully about your future needs before buying a cot bed. The main disadvantage arises if you have a second child soon after having your first. In this case you will need the cot again just when you have converted it into a bed and your first child is growing attached to it. Buying a new bed, banishing your toddler from the cot bed and rebuilding it into a cot as well as dealing with another new baby may be something you would rather avoid. Another possible disadvantage with cot beds is that as cots they often have fixed- rather than drop-sides (see page 64). You might also consider that you will have to buy your child a 'grown-up' bed at some point, so why not do it when he or she moves out of the cot? Cot beds are designed for children up to age six or so, but bear in mind the possibility that your status-conscious three- or four-year-old might start resenting having a baby bed when his or her friends have got 'proper' beds.

Bedside cots

You can buy cots with a removable side so that you can position the cot right next to your bed and there is no barrier between you and your baby. These cots have a base that you can adjust to a wide range of different heights, so that your and your baby's mattresses can be lined up (Mothercare★ produces a bedside cot with eight positions for £150). This makes night-time feeding easier. If you find it harder to relax with the baby so close, the cot can be easily converted into a conventional cot.

Unconventional cots

At the pricier end of the market are 'designer' cots, shaped to provide you and your child with advantages conventional cots do not have. The following are some examples.

- Jack Horner★ manufactures a **corner-shaped cot** that slots neatly into the corner of a room. It is roughly diamond-shaped – the side that fits into the corner is triangular, but the other side comes out into the room so there is quite a lot of space. This is a good option if you want as much free space as you can in the nursery without compromising on the size of the cot. It costs around £230.
- Stokke★ produces an **oval-shaped cot** that, once its life as a cot has finished, can be transformed into a junior bed (you have to pay extra for a bed kit), two chairs, a sofa or a play house. You can also pay extra for a kit that transforms the cot into a cradle for the first few months. Clearly you could get years of use out of a cot like this, but the same drawbacks could arise as with the cot bed (see above), and with an outlay of around £400 for the basic cot you will want to make sure the purchase is worthwhile.

- If you want an old-fashioned-looking iron cot, children's furniture specialist WigWam Kids★ sells one for £399.
- At the real luxury end of the market, you can buy a cot bed that turns into a stylish desk from the Natural Mat Company★. Made from American walnut and maple, it will set you back £1,750.

Travel cots
These can be handy for occasional use – see Chapter 5 for details.

> ❝ We put Nina's cot right in the middle of the room rather than against a wall. People think it looks odd but I think it gives her more of a sense of space when she is in the cot and it means we can approach the cot from either side to put her in or get her out. ❞
>
> Jan, mother of Nina, 8 months

Second-hand cots
Cots can be quite an expensive outlay, so many parents may be tempted to buy one second-hand or accept a hand-me-down from friends or relatives (see Chapter 1 for more on buying second-hand goods). If you do go for a used cot, it is important to consider the following advice.

- Avoid old family heirlooms (unless you are satisfied from a safety point of view – see the following points). The beautifully made cot you had when you were a baby may not meet current safety standards. These demand, for example, that cot bars are spaced closely enough to stop babies trapping their heads and that paint must be lead-free to prevent poisoning. Continuing with a family heirloom may compromise your child's safety.
- Measure the bar spacing and the distance between the top of the mattress and the top of the cot. The bar spacing needs to be between 2.5cm and 6.5cm and there must be at least 51cm between the top of the mattress and the top of the cot.
- Check that the drop-side mechanism (see page 64) works smoothly and stays reliably in the 'up' position.

- If there is any sign of peeling paint, strip and re-paint the cot (see 'Painting the nursery', at the end of this chapter).
- Remove any transfers on the inside of the cot that a baby could chew.
- Check that there are no footholds in the sides or cut-outs in the ends that could help a baby climb out.
- Check the mattress over carefully. You need to be sure that it is the correct size for the cot and that it is clean and has maintained its shape (see pages 75–76 for more on this). Unless you know the history of the mattress and are happy with its fit and condition, it is sensible to buy a new one.

Safety watch

Whether you use a cot from birth or transfer your baby to a cot after a couple of months, you will need to make up the bottom part of the cot with sheets and blankets folded under the mattress so that your baby sleeps in the 'feet to foot' position (see box on page 78).

Moses baskets

These are designed to provide your baby with a safe and snug sleeping place for the early weeks; one which you can take elsewhere with ease. Many parents find the sight of their tiny newborn in a full-sized cot a bit disconcerting and are happier with the tighter fit of a Moses basket. It is also argued that new babies feel more secure and sleep better in the enclosed space that these provide.

Usually made from natural palm leaf, Moses baskets are light. They have carry handles so you can move your sleeping baby if necessary. However, concerns have been raised by some medical professionals about the risk involved in doing this, after a number of cases of babies falling out of Moses baskets. The fact that the handles of some Moses baskets do not meet in the middle increases the risk of accidents. Although most incidents will not involve serious injury because babies will be falling from a low height, it is best to avoid carrying your baby around in the basket if possible, particularly if the handles do not meet in the middle. The basket also provides no protection for your baby if you slip or trip on the stairs.

You can place the Moses basket on the floor or, if you want your baby to be at a convenient height next to your bed, you can buy a fold-away stand (for around £20) to place the basket on. Check that this has a safety bar to prevent accidental closing. A PVC-covered foam mattress will normally be included with the basket, as well as a canopy or hood, lining, quilt and fancy 'skirt' (the Moses basket equivalent of a valance). Generally you can expect to pay £30–50 for a Moses basket with the associated trimmings (but not a stand), although there are pricier 'luxury' options available which will have extra padding and fancier attachments.

Pros:
✔ a light and portable sleeping place for your new baby
✔ when placed on a stand or other secure surface next to your bed, it enables you to reach your baby with ease for night-time feeds
✔ snug-fitting sides can help make some babies feel more secure
✔ fairly cheap choice if you have not yet decided what kind of cot you want and don't want to rush into anything
✔ provides a familiar sleeping place for your baby if you are staying overnight away from home.

Cons:
✘ some babies can find a cot hard to get used to after the confined space of a Moses basket – one of the reasons why many parents prefer to have their baby in a cot from birth
✘ an extra expense that is avoidable if you use a cot from the outset
✘ more expensive versions may look attractive but remember that your baby will be in the basket for a relatively short time (a couple of months or less is not uncommon) so it is easy to spend more than you need
✘ if you have other children, consider that a determined toddler or clumsy older child could knock the basket on its stand over
✘ handles may be unsuitable for carrying the basket with your baby inside and can also fray over time.

Carry cots

A carry cot is a sturdier alternative to a Moses basket although they share most of the same advantages and disadvantages. If you have a carry cot option on your pushchair you could use this as your baby's main sleeping place for the early weeks, although you may need to buy a mattress suitable for night-time sleeping (see pages 73–8). The clear disadvantage with this option is if you need to take your baby for a stroll and you want him or her to lie in the carry cot – unless you have the whole buggy contraption in your bedroom at night-time, you will spend a lot of time removing the carry cot from, and refitting it to, the base. You can buy separate carry cots, although they are not as widely available as Moses baskets. Choose one that is fairly lightweight as you may need to move your baby in it while he or she is sleeping (try Cheeky Rascals★).

Pros:
✔ as part of a pushchair, the multi-purpose nature of the carry-cot attachment (as a night-time as well as a daytime bed) is well liked by many parents
✔ generally more robust than Moses baskets so could be a useful investment for subsequent babies.

Cons:
✘ carry cots are usually placed on the ground or on a stable surface rather than on a stand, as with Moses baskets, so could be more problematic to position at an easily reachable height next to your bed
✘ depending on the model, they can be quite heavy and therefore cumbersome to move.

Cribs

Some parents like the traditional option of a crib for the early months. These usually have a gentle swinging or gliding action which helps to soothe some (but not all!) babies to sleep. They can also be locked into a fixed position for when your baby has settled. Avoid cribs or cradles that can't be stabilised like this, as you may find that the swinging motion doesn't suit your baby. Expect to pay around £60 for a basic crib plus more for crib-sized bedding. Check whether the basic price includes a mattress (retailers vary in what they offer). You can buy extras, such as crib bumpers and drapes that provide a canopy over the head of the crib. As with Moses baskets and carry cots, cribs are generally suitable from birth to around 3–4 months or when your baby starts to pull him- or herself upright.

Pros:
✔ swinging action can help calm many babies
✔ larger than Moses baskets so your baby has more room but can still feel snug. For the same reason, can be more suitable for bigger babies and can make the transition to a cot less disruptive
✔ convenient size and height for positioning next to parents' bed.

Cons:
✘ cribs are not portable
✘ some babies hate the swinging action and you won't normally find this out until it is too late. Even though it is gentle the swinging motion can simply roll a tiny baby back and forth, and this can be irritating and uncomfortable rather than soothing
✘ more expensive than Moses baskets – consider the fact your baby will be out of the crib before too long
✘ as with other cot alternatives, cribs are an extra expense that is avoidable if you use a cot from the outset.

Other sleeping places

There are alternatives to standard-looking Moses baskets and cribs. If you have delusions of grandeur for your baby, you may like the idea of him or her sleeping in a four-poster cradle, available from the Natural Mat Company★ for £229. You can also get cribs that are more like a hammock in style. Cheeky Rascals★ sells a cradle which hangs from the ceiling so it is free to sway in any direction; it is priced at £125.

Buying second-hand

Pre-cot sleeping units such as Moses baskets and cribs are sensible second-hand purchases. If you can borrow one or accept one as a hand-me-down, even better. They have many advantages for small babies but as you won't be needing one for long it could be worth saving your money to spend on a better-quality cot and mattress, which you will be using for longer.

If you do use a second-hand model, however, you need to be extra-careful about safety. On cribs, check that the locking pins are the correct ones for the model and fit neatly; on Moses baskets, check that the handles are in good condition. For both, check that the mattress has been kept clean and has maintained its shape – otherwise buy a new one.

Sharing your bed

Some parents don't use a cot, crib or Moses basket at all, preferring to have their baby sleep in bed with them. Although this can be comforting for you and your baby, a major research study has recently shown a link between cot death and bedsharing with babies under eight weeks old. The official advice from the Foundation for the Study of Infant Deaths (SIDS)* is that you should put your baby back in its own bed after you have cuddled or fed it if any of the following risk factors apply to you:

- your baby is under eight weeks old
- you or your partner smoke
- you have recently consumed alcohol or taken drugs
- you are extremely tired.

If you plan to sleep with your baby, don't let his or her head get covered by the pillow, use lightweight blankets rather than a duvet and make sure you place your baby in a position where he or she cannot fall out of bed.

Mattresses

Cots don't normally come with an inclusive mattress, so you will have to buy one separately. You might think that choosing a baby's mattress would be a fairly straightforward matter, but high-tech innovations have burst on to the baby-mattress market and the traditional choice between spring interior or simple foam has become somewhat more complicated. The 'buzz' words these days are 'detachable breathable top panels' and 'airflow systems'. Manufacturers and retailers use such terminology to convince customers of how effective their mattresses are at allowing air to circulate and flow through the mattress, reducing the effects of moisture build-up – the supposed result being a fresher mattress and a cooler, more comfortable baby.

Of course, all your baby really needs is a mattress that provides good support but is soft enough to be comfortable and is the right size for the cot. What may make a difference to parents, however, are factors such as how easy the mattress is to keep clean and how long it will be needed for. Mattresses that are completely covered with PVC or another wipe-clean surface are the most practical and hygienic. Aesthetics can come into the equation too – some mattresses simply look better than others. Many parents like the idea of a baby mattress that looks and feels like a mini-version of a traditional adult-sized mattress – for example, with springs and a quilted or 'ticking'-style covering – rather than a plastic-covered rectangle of foam.

Types of mattress

The two main types of mattress available are those with a foam core and those with a spring interior. You can also buy 'coir' mattresses, the core of which are made from natural coconut-shell fibres. Whatever you choose, the basic mattress core will be topped with one or more layers of other material – for instance, a waterproof covering and cotton padding.

Foam mattresses

Foam mattresses tend to be the least expensive kind. The simplest versions are made from a single layer of supportive foam completely covered with a wipe-clean, waterproof PVC cover. This cover protects your baby from dust mites (see box on page 77) as well as making the mattress easy to clean.

Some foam mattresses will be partially encased with PVC and will also have a section of ventilation holes, covered with fine mesh, positioned where your baby lies. These are designed to help your baby stay cool and to keep moisture – perspiration or dribble, for example – away from your baby (although they are not necessary and you shouldn't worry if your baby seems to lie everywhere other than over the holes). More complex and expensive foam mattresses will have the same or similar foam core with a waterproof cover, but also a removable panel on top made from 'breathable' fabric which, again, is designed to draw moisture away and so help prevent your baby from getting clammy and too hot. The main advantage with these is that they are easy to keep clean because you can remove this section to wash it.

Pros:
✔ generally easy to keep clean
✔ good value for money, at around £25–30 for a decent-quality but basic foam mattress
✔ can provide good support and resistance to denting.

Cons:
✘ some parents may not like the idea of the basic PVC-covered mattress because of concerns about clamminess
✘ mattresses with ventilation holes can be more effort to keep clean if your baby is a dribbler or possets a lot, because residue can gather in the holes and mesh (equally, there is no point in buying an expensive 'breathable' mattress if you're going to cover it with a PVC sheet to protect it from possetting and leaky nappies).

Spring-interior mattresses
These traditional mattresses have a coiled spring interior with layers of (usually) felt and foam padding. They often have a cotton cover on one side and PVC or other wipe-clean material on the other. The cotton cover can be sponged or vacuum cleaned. As with foam mattresses, you can also pay a bit extra for a spring mattress with a removable top panel, which will have moisture-reducing elements. Expect to pay around £45–£100 for a spring-interior mattress from a high-street nursery store.

Pros:

✔ many parents like the familiarity of a traditional spring mattress

✔ the wipe-clean side is the recommended surface for your baby to sleep on because of the practical advantages, but you have the option of flipping it over onto the cotton side if you prefer – for example, if it is hot and your baby feels clammy.

Cons:

✘ more expensive than foam

✘ the cotton side may be preferred for comfort but can be more difficult to keep clean (unless you buy a mattress with a removable panel).

Coir mattresses

These have a core of coconut fibre with other layers of different materials. The fibres are coated in latex for strength and protection. The natural fibre filling helps air to circulate through the mattress. These mattresses are available with a wipe-clean covering.

Pros:

✔ one of the firmest types of mattress

✔ tend to be longer lasting because they hold their shape well, so could be a sensible purchase if you want to use it for more than one child or if you are buying a cot bed which will be in use for some time by one child.

Cons:

✘ less widely available than foam or spring interior

✘ can be more expensive than both the above, at up to £155 for a cot-bed-sized mattress.

Points to consider before you buy

● Whichever mattress you decide on, make sure it is the right size for the cot (the size of cot the mattress will fit should be marked on the mattress and the cot). If the mattress is the wrong size your baby could be dangerously trapped in gaps between the cot and the mattress. As a rule, the gap between the mattress and the cot should be no more than 4cm.

- Mattresses tend to come in two basic sizes, to fit the equivalent sizes of cot generally available in the shops. If, however, you buy a cot that is smaller or larger than the norm, you can get mattresses specially made to fit your cot. Mothercare★, for example, offers a special-sized mattress service.
- Many parents accept that some mattress staining is inevitable with a baby or small child, but if you want to keep the mattress as hygienic and clean as possible, a PVC-covered mattress or one with a removable top panel that you can wash at a reasonably high temperature would be the most practical choice.
- Squeeze a selection of mattresses in the shop if you can, and choose one that feels firm rather than soft. To compare firmness, squeeze at the edges and at the centre. Your baby needs a mattress that provides good support and won't sag, rather than a mattress he or she can sink into.
- Look for a cot mattress that is 8–10cm thick. Anything thinner than this won't provide the support your baby needs. Thinner foam in particular can lose its shape and dent easily.
- Foam mattresses are lighter than other types and are therefore the easiest to lift when changing bedding. This can be an advantage if your movement is restricted, for example.
- If your family is prone to allergies such as asthma, a mattress that provides protection from dust mites (see box opposite) would be a sensible choice. Manufacturers and retailers who sell mattresses with anti-dust-mite properties will usually advertise the fact.

Mattress chemicals

In the early 1990s there were scares, prompted by the investigative TV programme *The Cook Report*, that chemical components in some mattresses caused babies to inhale small quantities of toxic gas. The suggestion was that there was a link between this and cot death. A Department of Health report prior to *The Cook Report*'s research had already ruled out evidence of a link, but the Foundation for the Study of Infant Deaths (SIDS)* commissioned further comprehensive research, which also failed to find any evidence for the theory.

> ## Dust mites
>
> Dust mites are microscopic organisms found in their millions in every home. One of their favourite habitats is the warmth and humidity of a mattress. It isn't so much the dust mites themselves that create a problem; it's their droppings. When these minuscule droppings are inhaled they can cause allergic reactions such as asthma and eczema in susceptible people. Babies up to the age of two are especially sensitive to developing allergies, particularly if there is a history of allergies in the family. Owing to parental concern about this possibility, combined with a rise in the number of children suffering from allergies, anti-dust-mite baby bedding has become increasingly popular as a means of trying to reduce the risk of allergies developing. (For more information, see *The Which? Guide to Asthma and Allergies*.)
>
> Dust mites are killed at a temperature of 60°C, so one option is to choose a mattress with a top layer that is washable at this temperature. Alternatively, go for one with a wipe-clean, waterproof surface.

Using the mattress for subsequent children

Retailers and manufacturers generally recommend that you buy a new mattress for each child. Cynics might say that this is because they want to sell as many mattresses as possible – but it is also true that a mattress can dip and sag with the weight of a growing baby and therefore might not provide an ideal sleeping surface for your next baby. A used mattress can also harbour dust mites, and babies who might be prone to allergies such as asthma may benefit from a new mattress if your existing one doesn't have anti-dust-mite protection. There have been reports that using a used mattress is linked to an increasing risk of cot death. The Foundation for the Study of Infant Deaths (SIDS)★, however, says that this is not the case and that what is important is that the mattress you use, wherever it is from, is in good condition. As long as the mattress has been kept reasonably clean, has maintained its shape and isn't sagging or damaged, it is acceptable for a subsequent baby to use and you don't need to spend money on a new one. If you do want the mattress for more than one child, then paying a bit extra for a better-quality one that you can also keep clean easily will be worth your while. It is also sensible to take care of the mattress by turning it regularly to maintain its shape. If you don't know the history of the mattress – for example, if someone has given it to you – check it carefully for sagging. (For more advice on second-hand goods, see pages 18–20.)

'Feet to foot' position

Cot death is very rare. Since new recommendations on how babies should be put to bed were introduced some years ago, incidents of cot death have declined substantially. The key thing to remember is that babies should always be put to sleep on their backs with their feet near the bottom end of the cot so that they can't shuffle down under the covers. The covers should be placed no higher than the chest and any surplus bedding should be tucked under the mattress. Your midwife or health visitor will show you how to tuck your baby in like this.

Bedding

The larger baby stores and catalogues will have a good selection of baby bedding for you to choose from. From simple sheets and blankets to baby sleeping bags, quilts for toddlers, cot bumpers and mattress protectors, the options are many and varied. Colours from white and traditional pastels to day-glo green and animal prints are available.

As with many other baby accessories, you don't actually *need* all that much. In terms of basic bedding, it makes sense to have a minimum of three bottom sheets, three top sheets and three blankets (all cellular, or one fleece and a couple of cellular – see page 81) – then in addition to those in use or in the wash you will always have one of each clean and ready if needed (if you'll be using baby sleeping bags, you'll only need the bottom sheets). Parents of babies who posset a lot may want to have more changes of bedding at hand. Buy the basic amount to start with, perhaps with a couple of spares, and see how you get on. You can buy small sheets and blankets for Moses baskets, prams, carry cots and cribs as well as larger sheets for cots and cot beds.

Sheets

These are usually sold in packs of two and you can buy them fitted or flat. Expect to pay around £10 for a pack of cot sheets; less for crib or pram sheets and more for cot bed sheets.

- **Fitted** – these are very useful, especially as your baby gets older and moves around in the cot more. A fitted sheet won't ruffle and come away from the mattress as a result of a squirming baby. The main disadvantage with fitted sheets is that if the mattress you have bought is quite stiff and heavy, fitting the sheets may be cumbersome (although you'll soon get well-practised). Lighter, foam-based mattresses tend to be easier to fit sheets on to. Fitted sheets tend to be made of cotton jersey or terry (fine towelling cotton/polyester mix). Both have an advantage in that they don't need to be ironed (although ironing cot sheets, whatever they are made from, is probably not a priority for most busy parents!).
- **Flat** – these tend to be used as a top sheet in combination with a blanket, although they are fine for use as a bottom sheet too. Generally they are more awkward to put on as a bottom sheet than fitted sheets, although many people prefer them. Flat sheets tend to be made either from flannelette or plain cotton. Plain cotton has the advantage that it can be washed at higher temperatures, although it doesn't feel as soft as flannelette.

Tip

You can cut up full-sized sheets to make smaller sheets for cots and other baby sleeping units. Just make sure edges aren't frayed, as little fingers can get caught up in the threads (you could just turn over the edges and whizz along with the sewing machine).

Mattress clips

If you use flat bottom-sheets for the cot or cot bed but always find them ruffled up in the morning, you can get special clips that go under the mattress and hold the sheet taut. They can also be useful if you use a full-sized sheet on the mattress – you just fold the sheet under the mattress and clip on the fasteners. The clips are available from JoJo Maman Bébé*, or try department stores.

Temperature guide

Small babies cannot regulate their body temperature very well so it is important not to let the room get too hot or too cold. Don't put your baby to sleep next to a radiator or heater or near a sunny window on a hot day. A comfortable room temperature for a baby is around 18°C.

If you feel uneasy about temperature, nursery thermometers are widely available. They are not expensive (around £3) but are not a necessity either – trusting your instincts is probably just as good. Get into the habit of feeling your baby's tummy to make sure he or she isn't too hot or cold, and check for perspiration.

The amount of bedding you use should vary according to the season and temperature of the room. If you are worried about using too much or too little bedding and want to use a nursery ther-mometer to gauge this, use the following temperature guide.

24°C – sheet only
21°C – sheet plus one layer of blanket
18°C – sheet plus two layers of blanket
15°C – sheet plus three layers of blanket

(Note that a folded blanket counts as two layers of blanket.)

Safety watch

The advice from the Foundation for the Study of Infant Deaths (SIDS)* is that **cot duvets**, **quilts** and **pillows** should not be used until your baby is one year old. This is because they carry an increased risk of suffocation and overheating in younger babies.

Blankets

The types of blankets most commonly available are cotton cellular, acrylic cellular and fleece.

- **Cotton cellular** – these are 100-per-cent cotton. Their cellular structure (they are loosely woven such that they have small holes throughout – note that this design is not meant to reduce the risk of suffocation) means that they are warm in winter and cool in summer, so they are good for year-round use. They are also lightweight. They have the advantage of being washable at higher temperatures than fleece or acrylic.
- **Acrylic cellular** – these are extra-lightweight and quick drying, with the same year-round usefulness as the cotton cellular type. They are generally similar in price to cotton cellular blankets, although they tend not to be as soft on the skin as cotton or fleece.
- **Fleece** – made from 100-per-cent polyester, fleece blankets are soft and easy to wash and dry. You can buy brightly coloured designs which often have attractive appliqué motifs. Fleece blankets tend to be more expensive than other types – at the time of writing, Mothercare★ was charging £12.99 for a fleece blanket and £9 for cotton cellular and acrylic cellular.

Other bedding and cot accessories

Sleeping bags

Baby sleeping bags are becoming increasingly popular in the UK and have been so for a long time in continental Europe. They usually have a full-length front zip or poppers at the shoulders and sometimes a zip at the side with sleeveless arm-holes. Rather than tucking your baby up at night under sheets and blankets, you simply zip or popper him or her into the bag. The bags normally come in either baby- or toddler-sized. They are usually quite lightweight with minimal padding. If the bag has a tog rating, choose low – anything higher than 2.5 togs could prove too warm for your baby. Likewise, avoid bags with a hood or with full-length sleeves. Sleeping bags are now widely available from nursery stores and catalogues, and you can also order direct from specialist baby-sleeping-bag companies such as Grobag★ and Snugger★.

Pros:

✔ no covers to throw off, so your baby stays warm all night

✔ takes away some of the worry about how many sheets or blankets you should be using (although you still need to be aware that your baby shouldn't get too hot – if the room is very warm, your baby may need a light sheet rather than the sleeping bag) and you won't need to get anxious about your baby's head being covered with bedding

✔ something familiar to your baby which you can take away with you if you are staying elsewhere.

Cons:

✘ older babies and toddlers may find the bags constricting because they can't move around the cot as freely as if they had conventional bedding. Standing babies and toddlers may shuffle along upright in their bag, get entangled and fall on to the sides of the cot

✘ sleeping bags can get grubby simply because you are unlikely to have changes of sleeping bag at hand in the same way that you would have clean bedding at the ready – buy two if you can

✘ may be harder to modify for slight variations in temperature

✘ some retailers recommend that you avoid using these for smaller newborns (under 3.5kg, or 7lb 12oz) who can be 'swamped' by them, so it is best to wait for a few weeks if you have a small baby.

Quilts, duvets and pillows

Once your baby reaches one year of age (see box on page 81), it is fine to replace his or her baby blankets and top sheets with a cot quilt or duvet. You can get simple, understated designs as well as bright-and-breezy 'all singing, all dancing' quilts with built-in features, such as animal ears that squeak or crinkle when you press them. Pillows can also be safely used from the age of one, but don't feel you have to buy one – your baby will be used to sleeping without one and may even not want it in the cot.

Pros:
✔ getting used to a quilt in the cot may help with the eventual move to a quilt-covered bed
✔ easy to make up – no more fussing with blankets and top sheets.

Cons:
✗ your baby may have grown attached to his or her blankets and may not like the idea of a quilt
✗ an unnecessary expense – he or she will be moving to a bed soon enough so you could easily keep the 'baby bedding' going until then.

Coverlets and comforters

A coverlet or comforter is a lightweight baby version of a quilt that can safely be used for babies under one year old because it does not have the soft padding of a standard quilt (although if your new baby is under 3.5 kg, or 7lb 12oz, some retailers recommend you wait until he or she is this weight before you use one). It is as warm as a sheet and blanket combined.

Pros:
✔ less bedding to deal with at night-time
✔ usually part of a coordinated nursery range, so if you want to match your baby's cot bedding with the curtains, you can.

Cons:
✗ tend to be more expensive than a sheet and blanket (Mothercare's★ Winnie-the-Pooh range coverlet is £35)
✗ you will probably need sheets and blankets anyway (as spares or for cold nights, for example) so it might be worth just keeping to these.

Baby sheepskin fleeces

These are basically mini sheepskin rugs. They are designed to be soft and comforting for babies to lie on, and many parents who have used them feel that they calm and soothe newborns. If you buy one, make sure it is specifically for baby use.

Pros
- ✔ cool in the summer and warm in the winter
- ✔ many babies do seem to like the feel of them.

Cons:
- ✘ not recommended for use as a sleeping surface for babies who roll over on to their fronts because of the risk of the soft fur surface restricting breathing
- ✘ there is a possibility that they can harbour dust mites (more so than normal blankets) so you should wash them regularly in hot water, particularly if your baby is prone to allergies.

Cot bumpers

These are soft pads that are tied to the top and around the upper section of the sides of the cot, designed to give babies some protection from the hard sides. Bumpers are often sold as part of a coordinated bedding range so can be especially appealing to parents who want a matching style for the nursery. However, they definitely come into the 'optional accessory' category. (There have been concerns in the past that they can make babies too hot, encouraging the risk of cot death – however, the most recent research has shown no adverse effects.)

Pros:
- ✔ if you have a wriggly baby, bumpers do help prevent any little bumps in the night against the cot frame
- ✔ they help stop dummies from falling through the gaps in the cot bars so are a useful way of keeping anything your baby is particularly attached to within reach
- ✔ some have touchy-feely materials or playthings attached so have the potential to provide a degree of in-cot entertainment.

Cons:

✗ the lifespan of bumpers can be quite limited – putting your baby in the feet-to-foot position to go to sleep means they are redundant in the early days, when your baby's head shouldn't be near the top end of the cot anyway, and once he or she gets more mobile and starts pulling up they have to be removed from the cot in case they are used as a lever to climb out

✗ they need to be securely tied to the cot with the attached ties and these ties should be short to avoid your baby becoming tangled or chewing on them. (These days any bumper you buy from a reputable shop is likely to have short ties, but check hand-me-down or second-hand bumpers: if the ties seem long – say, over 20cm per tie – trim them down, making sure there are no frayed edges.)

Cat nets

A cat net is a strong mesh net that can be fitted over a cot and helps to protect your baby against cats climbing into it. They are available from many nursery stores and online retailers for around £10 – try The Baby Catalogue★ or contact the main manufacturer, Clippasafe★, for details of stockists. You can also get cat nets for prams (see Chapter 6).

Protective bedding

See page 213 for information about bedding to protect the mattress from bed-wetting, once your child reaches toilet-training age.

Sleeping position aids

Anxiety about cot death, and the recommendation that babies should sleep on their backs with their feet at the foot of the cot, have led to a number of cot products coming on to the market that are designed to alleviate parents' anxieties about sleeping positions.

One such product is the Safababy Sleeper (available from Blooming Marvellous★). This is a covered barrier that, once placed inside the cot, shortens the length of your baby's sleeping area so that he or she is always in the 'feet to foot' position. You secure the separator on top of the bedding and attach it to the sides of the cot so that your baby can't slide underneath the blankets. It also prevents your baby from kicking hard cot ends.

Another sleeping position aid is the Air Flow Sleep Positioner (available by mail order from JoJo Maman Bébé★), which is a polyester foam-rounded frame designed to encourage the safer habit of sleeping on the back. You place your baby on the frame to sleep and the softly rounded sides prevent him or her from turning over.

Pros:

✔ can provide some peace of mind for parents who are particularly anxious about their baby's sleeping position.

Cons:

✘ they are an unnecessary extra – it is not hard to tuck your baby in at the 'feet to foot' position once you know how to do it and, for babies who tend to roll naturally on to their fronts to sleep, the advice from the Foundation for the Study of Infant Deaths (SIDS)★ is that as long as you place them on their back each night and turn them during your normal checks, there is no need to be anxious

✘ any sleeping aid that your baby could use to lever him- or herself up with must be removed as soon as your baby is capable of pulling up – so you need to be vigilant

✘ remembering to position the sleeping aid in the cot each night in addition to washing, feeding, changing, tucking in and settling down is one more night-time procedure you could well do without.

Other nursery furniture and accessories

Changing tables

A baby changing table (sometimes called a baby changing unit or dresser) is a piece of equipment designed so that you can change your baby's nappies at a comfortable waist-height rather than kneeling and bending over to change him or her on the floor. They either have an integral padded changing surface or you have to place a separate changing mat on top. They come with storage units or shelves underneath so you can keep nappies, wipes and any other paraphernalia you may use all in one place, a handy distance from where you are changing your baby. Many have a plastic baby bath as part of the unit so that you can bathe your baby at a comfortable waist-height too. The changing surface covers the bath when not in use. Some also have accessory trays at hand-height, alongside the changing surface, so you can keep smaller bits and bobs such as cotton wool or nappy creams at close hand.

There are two main types of table: 'furniture'-style and open-shelf style. Both are widely available from a range of outlets.

Furniture-style units

At the more expensive end of the market, these tend to be made up of a cupboard and drawers housed in a wooden waist-height unit and topped with a wide changing surface. You place a changing mat on top of this surface. The idea is that these units look like stylish pieces of furniture in their own right, which you can use for storage beyond the nappy-changing months. Fashionable 'Shaker' designs are popular at the time of writing. Some units are big enough to use them to store your baby's clothes as well as changing materials.

Pros:

✔ you can carry on using these for clothes or toy storage even when your baby is well past the nappy stage. In other words, they can be used as permanent items of furniture – so although they can be quite expensive you can get use out of them for years to come

✔ they often come as part of a set of nursery furniture so, if you want a coordinated look for the nursery, you can get a cot, wardrobe and shelves to match.

Cons:

✘ they can be pricey (expect to pay £200–350 for this style of unit). In terms of what they are basically designed for – namely as a piece of equipment to help you change your baby with minimum fuss – a more basic unit will do the job just as well for a fraction of the price

✘ some can be quite bulky so are not suitable if space is at a premium

✘ think about whether you really want the piece of equipment you change your baby on to stay in your child's room for years to come. Perhaps by the time your baby is a toddler or older you will want to change the look of the nursery and might see other items of furniture that will suit your needs and wants better.

Open-shelf-style units

These units usually have two wide shelves or storage containers, with a further changing shelf on top. Some are functional-looking 'trolley'-style units with casters so you can move the unit around if you want. Many of these include a plastic bath incorporated into the unit and have an integral changing mat. Others are made of wood and may have a longer-lasting appeal because the shelves can be used for toys or books later on.

Pros:

✔ at around £50–100 these are far cheaper than the furniture-style units

✔ tend to take up less space – if you are short on space, the less bulky the changing table the better

✔ open shelving can be more practical because you can easily see and reach for nappies, wipes, etc. rather than having to search around in cupboards and drawers.

Cons:

✘ many designs don't have the same 'staying power' as furniture-style units, because they aren't as multi-functional, and you are less likely to want to use one for general storage later on

✘ units that come with a baby bath can seem like a good idea, but because you have to fill and empty the bath by hand it can be a bit messy (and there's a fair chance of making a mess en route from the bathroom!). You will have a convenient waist-height surface upon which to bathe your baby in the early days, but placing a plastic baby bath on any other stable surface or putting it in the bath itself is probably a more practical option for most people. (See pages 46–50 for more about baby baths.)

Other types of changing table

- **Cot-top changers** – this type is a useful 'halfway house' between a changing unit and a simple changing mat. It is a rigid plastic rectangle with a padded changing mat that you place widthways on top of the cot at changing time. It means you can change the baby at a comfortable height but also save on the space that an ordinary changing unit takes up. At around £20–35 or so, these are also far cheaper than standard changing units. Try Babies 'R' Us★ or the Boots★ website.

- **Fold-away changers** – this style of changer is often seen in the toilets or baby-changing rooms of restaurants and shops. Generally made from plastic and having the appearance of a curved, tray-like shelf, the changer needs to be firmly fixed to the wall because it has no underneath support. When not in use, you fold it up on to the wall. It is useful if you are short of space, but cheaper options are available and because these changers don't have storage space you can't keep your bits and pieces at hand. An example of this kind of changer is the Redinap★ Ezeechanger, at £125; this is also marketed as useful for parents with movement difficulties (see pages 21–2).

Do you really need one?

The answer to this question has to be 'no'. A changing table is a non-essential item that can certainly be described as a luxury rather than a 'must-have'. Changing your baby on a wipe-clean mat on the floor is straightforward and practical, and the equipment only costs a few pounds. (See pages 40–1 for more about changing mats.) You can move the mat around the house, so you can change your baby at the most convenient place for you, or you could have two mats – one in the baby's room and one in the living room – so you don't have to move anything. Changing tables tend to tie you down to changing your baby in one place. If your changing table is in the baby's room, trudging there each time your baby needs a fresh nappy can become a form of exercise you can well do without, especially in the early days. Portable units on lockable casters provide a bit more mobility, but in reality even these will probably end up 'parked' in the same place. Bear in mind that you may not use the changing surface part of the table for very long anyway – once your baby can move around you may feel safer abandoning using the table altogether because of the danger of his or her falling off (see box overleaf).

That said, many people do find changing tables very useful. If you have a bad back and prefer to avoid crouching on the floor, a changing table can be a lifesaver because you are changing your child at a height to suit you. They can also help you keep all your baby's essentials in one place: you won't be searching around for a packet of wipes or the nappy cream because (if you are using the table as it is meant to be used) everything will be stored there.

What to look for

If you decide a changing table would be useful for you, bear the following points in mind.

- Try to choose a table with a safety strap. Even though you should never leave your baby unattended on a changing unit, a safety strap will give you extra peace of mind.
- If there is an incorporated changing mat, check that the sides of the mat are reasonably ridged. Anything that can help keep your baby secure is a bonus – just in case he or she does a flip when you are not concentrating.
- Units with hand-height accessory trays as well as storage space underneath the changing surface are the most useful.
- Think about whether you want your unit to be used for general storage later on, in which case it is worth considering one of the more expensive furniture-style units, or whether you are happy to have it as a temporary nursery item.

Safety watch

As with placing your baby on any high surface, there is an increased risk of accidents with changing tables. You should never leave your baby unattended on a changing table. Even small babies can move in ways you wouldn't expect and can fall off. If you have to answer the phone or door while your baby is on the table, take him or her with you.

Nursery lighting

You can buy lights specially designed for use in your baby's bedroom, which emit a soft light. Although an ordinary lamp or ceiling light is perfectly adequate for use in the nursery, many parents and babies like the soothing effect of a soft nightlight or lights that shine projected images such as clouds or nursery characters on to the wall and ceiling. As well as possibly helping your baby to go to sleep, a soft light can be useful for tending to him or her in the middle of the night. Some types can also be handy later on if your child dislikes the dark, as many do. You can choose from a range of different types of nursery lights. Those you are most likely to come across are the following.

- **Cot lights** – these are attached to the cot and emit a battery-powered soft light. Many are sound-sensitive and light up when your baby cries, or you can switch them to be on all night. The more elaborate versions also play lullabies or 'nature sounds' as well as providing light. At the top end of the market are cot lights that project rotating images around the ceiling to the tune of lullabies – for example, the Tomy★ Lullaby Dream Show light (widely available from nursery stores and the baby sections of some toy shops). The price range for these lights is around £10–30.
- **Plug-in nightlights** – these are small, round or oval lights that you plug directly into the wall socket. Some have light sensors so they come on automatically at night and go off at daylight. The price range is around £4–10.
- **Light-effect bedside lights** – you can buy bedside lights that project rotating images round the room, or ones that automatically fade out over a 15-minute period so that you have a brighter light to start with while you are settling your baby down. The price range is around £20–33.
- **'Instant' lights** – these are battery-powered, cord-free, flat, rounded lights that you can fix on to the wall or place on any convenient surface. You push them down to activate them. The price range is around £6 for a pack of two.

Although not designed specifically for use in a baby's or child's room, dimmer switches are also a very effective way of lighting the nursery; if you have one there should be no need for a nightlight as well, unless you want the automatic on–off element that some of these provide. Some models of baby monitor also come with a nightlight. If you decide to buy a plug-in nightlight, bear in mind that an innocuous-looking light rather than one with a children's character printed on it is probably the best choice if you want to reduce the chances of a curious child playing around with the socket. (For more on safety in the home, see Chapter 7.)

> **"**I lined the nursery curtains with blackout fabric – good if you want your baby to give you a bit of a lie-in in the mornings. If you get them used to the dark as newborns it's less likely to be a problem later on.**"**
>
> Kate, mother of Silas, 13 months

Other nursery accessories

When you first start choosing items for your new baby, you will be entering a world full of products you are unlikely to have even heard of during your pre-baby days, and you will need an explanation of what they are for before you buy. This is particularly the case with fixtures and fittings for the nursery. The items on the following list may appeal to some parents – although, as many of them are sold as part of a coordinated nursery range (see overleaf), they may well be chosen for their appearance rather than their usefulness.

Fashions and tastes in nursery styles change along with product ranges. At the time of writing, for example, Mothercare* had dropped some of its 'fancy' non-essential nursery fittings such as cot tidies and valances (see below) from its range in favour of a simpler nursery look.

- **Nappy stacker** – a hanging holdall, usually made from cotton/polyester with 'stacked' open pockets designed to keep a large pile of nappies neatly stored and easy to reach.
- **Cot tidy** – a flat, fabric holdall that fastens on to the side of the cot and which has open pockets for small toys and books.
- **Cot drape** – a light curtain that hangs above the head of the cot on a drape rod and is designed to give a romantic, old-fashioned look to the nursery.
- **Cot valance** – fancy frills to cover the cot mattress.
- **Nursing chair** – a chair with low, padded arm-rests and a gliding/rocking motion designed to provide a comfortable place for feeding and soothing your baby. On some models

you can position the chair in a variety of reclining positions. You can expect to pay around £250–350 for a nursing chair plus an extra £100 if you want a matching footstool.

> **"**Put as many shelves as you can up in your baby's room. They can provide loads of extra space for storing toys and other bits and pieces. Make sure you have a couple of low-level shelves too, or a small bookcase. Amy has just started selecting her own books to look at from the bookshelf and she seems to take real pleasure in being able to reach and pick and choose what she wants without my help.**"**
>
> Jenny, mother of Amy, 20 months

Coordinated furnishings

Most parents want their new baby's room to look attractive and newly decorated – this is, understandably, all part of the nesting process. Manufacturers and retailers tap into this instinct and produce ready-matched nursery ranges, so you can buy the wallpaper to match the curtains that go with the cot bumper and the lampshade, and so on. Catalogues from retailers such as Mothercare★ and Babies 'R' Us★ are packed with photographs of rooms 'dressed' from head to toe in the latest nursery ranges. These can look very tempting, but when you stop to think about how much extra the 'bought-in' coordinated look can cost, the attractiveness may wane. It is true that most people are unlikely to get everything from one range and will pick and choose the items they most want or like. However, in the quest for the perfect nursery, coordinated ranges do tend to encourage you to buy items you don't really need, and it can be tempting to think along the lines of 'Mmm, that matching cot tidy could be useful and it's only another £15.' Then the costs really start to mount up.

What you could spend on furnishing

Below is an example of how much you could spend if you really went to town. The prices are based on mid-range furnishings from a leading mass-market nursery retailer, so actually give a fairly conservative estimate – you would obviously end up paying a lot more if you opted for a range from the 'designer' end of the nursery-furnishings market.

Basics

Cot:	£130
Mattress:	£65
Cot bedding:	£50
Changing mat:	£8
Total cost:	**£253**

Extras

Nursing chair (definitely a luxury item):	£340
Baby/child wardrobe:	£275
Changing unit:	£100
Over-cot mobile	£30
Cot bumper:	£33
Curtain and tie-backs:	£27
Black-out curtain linings:	£15
Lampshade:	£15
Cot tidy:	£13
Nappy stacker:	£10
Decorative cushion:	£10
Wallpaper border:	£9
Room thermometer:	£3
Total cost:	**£880**

Grand total:	**£1,133**

All the items in the 'extras' list are things you don't really need but that may prove useful or may simply be attractive to you. The point is that even picking and choosing a selection of items from this list can help to push the cost of furnishing the nursery right up. Remember too that you are also likely to be buying extra items for the early weeks when your baby will be sleeping in your room – a Moses basket with a stand and bedding, for example, can cost around £90. Other items not included in the above list but that you can also buy as part of a range are wallpaper, a rug, and a cot quilt and pillow (for use when your baby reaches one year of age).

Looking ahead

Apart from the cost connotations, there is another good argument for keeping the room décor and furnishings fairly simple. Although it is hard to imagine it when your baby is small, before too long he or she could be developing strong tastes in how his or her room should look, and this may well not include the Winnie-the-Pooh fixtures and fittings you decorated the room with before the birth. If you want to avoid the pressure to redecorate the room in three years' time, it is worth thinking about steering clear of character furnishings. No matter how cute they look to you now, they may just spell 'baby' to a pre-schooler desperate to be big. Likewise, think carefully before buying child-sized wardrobes and chests of drawers. As your baby grows into a toddler, space for toys and all the other paraphernalia that seem to mount up when you have children will be at a premium, so the more storage space you have the better.

Painting the nursery

If you want to give the nursery walls a new look, keeping them plain is the most sensible option. It will be easier to match other items in the room to them if you want a coordinated look, and you can also decorate them with pictures, stencils or friezes. Choose vinyl wallpapers or a water-based vinyl silk or eggshell paint. Water-based paints contain fewer solvents than oil-based paints, although they aren't particularly easy to clean. If you are going to paint the nursery, do it well before your baby moves in, so he or she isn't exposed to any fumes.

All standard paints are now lead-free, but you should be careful if you are placing an old, painted item of furniture in the nursery – the old paint may have a high lead content which, if it is peeling or flaking, could find its way into your baby's mouth at some point. You should be able to buy a test kit for lead-based paint from your local builder's merchant.

If you have access to the Internet, you can get some interesting nursery decorating ideas from DIY retailers' websites – try Homebase*.

“I spent ages sanding and varnishing the floorboards in the nursery. It looked great but I really wish I'd bought a carpet. It would have made Joe's room a more comfortable place to play now that he is crawling, and when he was smaller I was always having to put something under him before laying him down on the floor.”

Fiona, mother of Joe, 10 months

Websites

Babies 'R' Us	www.babiesrus.co.uk
The Baby Catalogue	www.thebabycatalogue.com
Blooming Marvellous	www.bloomingmarvellous.co.uk
Boots	www.boots.com
Cheeky Rascals	www.cheekyrascals.co.uk
Clippasafe	www.clippasafe.co.uk
Foundation for the Study of Infant Deaths	www.sids.org.uk/fsid
Grobag	www.grobag.com
Homebase	www.homebase.co.uk
Jack Horner	www.jack-horner.co.uk
JoJo Maman Bébé	www.jojomamanbebe.co.uk
Mothercare	www.mothercare.co.uk
The Natural Mat Company	www.naturalmat.com
Redinap	www.redinap.co.uk
Snugger	www.snuggeruk.com
Stokke	www.stokke.com
Tomy	www.tomy.co.uk
Urchin	www.urchin.co.uk
WigWam Kids	www.wigwamkids.co.uk

Nursery checklist

Item	Notes
Moses basket	
Carry cot	
Crib	
Standard cot	
Cot bed	
Bedside cot	
Other type of cot	
Mattress	
Travel cot (Ch 5)	
Sheets	
Blankets	
Sleeping bag	
Duvet/quilt/pillow	
Coverlet/comforter	
Sheepskin fleece	
Cot bumpers	
Cat net	
Protective bedding (Ch 8)	
Sleeping position aids	
Changing table/unit	
Nursing chair	
Lighting	
Other nursery accessories	

Chapter 4

Feeding equipment

Thinking about what your baby drinks and eats can easily become an obsession. From the first gulps from the breast or bottle to the refusals later on to eat anything green, worrying that he or she is having too little or too much is a parental emotion hard to avoid.

Whatever your baby's dietary habits and mode of getting nutrition, you are sure to be besieged by a wealth of feeding products and equipment from the word go. Even if you are breast-feeding, so don't need to think about formula milk and bottles for the time being, there is still the option of a range of breast-feeding accessories – which may be useful or useless depending on your personal preferences and experiences. And once your baby goes on to solids, at some point you'll probably be fretting that you're not doing the right thing because you buy packets or jars of food rather than making your own. This chapter includes information about shop-bought baby food and what to look for on the labels. With most feeding products and equipment there is likely to be a degree of trial and error in finding out what suits you and your baby best.

Bottles and teats

A baby's bottle seems such a simple and uncomplicated item, yet getting the right bottle for their baby is a task many parents find troublesome. That's because different bottles – or more specifically, teats – suit different babies, and the one that your friend's baby happily uses won't necessarily be the one that yours will take to. Many parents do hit the jackpot first time, either because they are lucky or because their baby isn't fussy. For others, an experimental process will be necessary. This may be especially the case for mothers trying to wean their baby off the breast and on to the bottle.

If you will be bottle-feeding more or less from the birth, you'll need to buy six bottles. Even if you are breast-feeding or planning to, there is a good chance that you will buy bottles at some point during your baby's first year, so it's worth familiarising yourself with the advantages and disadvantages of different types of bottle, and perhaps having one or two to hand in case you need them.

Types of bottle

The basic choice is between standard and wide-necked bottles. Within these two categories there are bottles with added features, such as an easy-to-hold shape or heat-sensitive material. Teats normally come with the bottle but you can also buy them separately. It pays to have more teats than bottles, as they will need replacing (for more on teats, see pages 102–3). The usual amount of milk a bottle will hold is 250ml, although you can get smaller bottles for new babies.

Standard bottles

These are the narrow, cylindrical bottles that are a familiar sight. You can buy them plain or decorated with various babyish designs. They will fit a range of standard teats and either have self-seal lids or, less commonly these days, come with sealing discs, which you use to seal the milk in the bottle when you go out (this sort also have lids but these are not leak-proof, unless specifically designed to be so).

Pros:

✔ most widely available

✔ most likely to fit accessories such as bottle coolers and sterilisers

✔ least expensive type of bottle.

Cons:

✘ bottles with sealing discs can be an irritation – self-sealing lids are far less fiddly if you are taking a bottle out with you

✘ the narrow neck means they can be trickier to fill than wide-necked versions, so are more likely to result in milk powder spills.

Wide-necked bottles

Pioneered by the manufacturer Avent, these are shorter and fatter than standard bottles but take the same amount of milk. They usually take silicone rather than latex teats and will often have a self-sealing lid.

Pros:
- ✔ easy to clean and fill
- ✔ some are designed to have anti-colic properties, as babies are less likely to gulp down air with their milk (see below).

Cons:
- ✘ less versatile, in the sense that once you start using a wide-necked bottle you'll probably be sticking to bottles and accessories made by one or two manufacturers
- ✘ take up more space – for instance, you may not be able to fit as many bottles in a steriliser.

Unusually shaped bottles

Some bottles are shaped to be easier for little hands to hold. Oval-shaped bottles with a hole in the middle for fingers to grip are widely available. You can also buy bottles with rounded ridges along the sides and 'nipped in' waists. Wide-necked, angle-shaped bottles, on the other hand, are designed to be anti-colic. Because the top of the bottle is at an angle the milk always stays in the teat, so there's less likelihood of the baby swallowing air. The manufacturers say that this reduces colic.

Pros:
- ✔ easy-grip bottles are useful for encouraging older babies to drink unaided
- ✔ angle-shaped bottles are worth a try if your baby has colic.

Cons:
- ✘ some unusually shaped bottles can be more difficult to clean, as milk residue gathers in the nooks and crannies – you may need to buy a special bottle-brush
- ✘ they may not fit in your steriliser
- ✘ the main potential advantage of anti-colic bottles is fairly short-lived as colic is unusual after three months of age.

Heat-sensitive bottles

A fairly recent innovation, these bottles have an in-built temperature sensor which changes colour if the milk is too hot.

Pros:

✔ may be useful if you are particularly anxious about giving your baby too-hot milk.

Cons:

✘ arguably unnecessary – using the inside of your wrist to test milk temperature is a time-honoured method that works well enough for most people.

Bottle 'sets' or 'systems'

Some manufacturers produce bottle sets which include attachments such as handles and trainer spouts, which you can fit on to the bottles when your baby reaches the appropriate stage. The idea is that you stick with the same bottles from birth to weaning and simply customise them for your baby's needs and capabilities.

Pros:

✔ versatile

✔ good value for money if you stick with the same bottle system.

Cons:

✘ your baby may prefer a 'non-system' type of bottle or spout, in which case the bottle system isn't good value for money or versatile

✘ you may be buying into the particular manufacturer's range of products so may be less willing to experiment with other brands.

Disposable bottles

These are not so much disposable bottles as disposable, sterilised bags that fit into a bottle. You fit them into the bottle, fill them with milk, and throw them away when your baby has finished.

Pros:

✔ convenient to use when out or on holiday as there is no need for a steriliser.

Cons:

✘ expensive if used daily

✘ you may not feel comfortable with another disposable item – you'll be generating enough waste from other baby-related paraphernalia.

Glass bottles

You may be surprised to hear that you can buy glass feeding bottles. They are not widely available but parents who are concerned about chemicals in plastic bottles often opt to buy them. Most baby feeding bottles in the UK are made from polycarbonate plastic derived from a chemical called Bisphenol A (BPA). Studies on animals have shown that low levels of BPA can affect fertility and the reproductive organs. The BPA in plastic bottles can be released after bottle-brushing, dishwashing or sterilisation. The government says that BPA as currently used by manufacturers is unlikely to be a concern to health and that there is no need to change the type of bottles you use. However, if you are worried you can minimise the risk of the chemical being released by replacing old bottles with new ones on a regular basis, or by buying glass bottles (available from Green Baby*).

Types of teat

The type of teat you choose may make a difference to how well your baby feeds, so you might need to experiment with different types.

Latex or silicone?

Teats are made from either latex or silicone. Latex tends to feel softer but, if you can get your baby to take one, silicone teats are more practical for parents. Silicone is more durable and can withstand more easily the barrage of washing and sterilising that is necessary to keep a teat clean. Rubber teats can become sticky and weak after repeated use and will need replacing more often. Wide-necked bottles normally only take silicone teats while standard bottles can take either.

Traditional or orthodontic?

The usual shape for a teat is either the traditional bell shape or a bulbous, orthodontic shape that is meant to resemble more closely the shape of a nipple and the contours of your baby's mouth. Again, you may need to try both to find which type your baby prefers. Some teats have anti-colic valves, which are dents or holes in the teat that are designed to reduce the amount of air your baby takes in with the milk. Some also have 'dimples' on the teat which are designed to mimic the feel of a real nipple.

Flow rate

How fast the milk goes into your baby's mouth depends on the number and type of holes in the tip of the teat. You need to choose a teat with a 'flow rate' that suits your baby. Teats range from slow-flow through to medium- and fast-flow, for babies who can cope with more milk with each suck. The flow rate suitable for your baby is not necessarily related to his or her age – some new babies may prefer a medium or fast-flow teat, as they can get tired if they have to suck hard to make the milk flow. You can also buy variable flow teats, which suit babies of all ages as the flow is determined by how hard they suck. You probably need to change the teat to a slower-flow one if your baby is spluttering his or her milk out and choking, or to a faster one if he or she is sucking hard but seems to be getting frustrated.

Bottle accessories

You will need a bottle-brush to clean your bottles properly before sterilising and a teat-brush to get into the tips of the teats. Optional extras include:

- **dishwasher basket** – a small basket for keeping your teats, dummies, etc. in one place inside the dishwasher (otherwise they can fall through the gaps)
- **bottle-drying rack** – for easy drying of hand-washed bottles and teats
- **bottle cooler bags** – insulated bags that keep milk fresh when you're out and about; single or multi-bottle sizes are available (if you have a changing bag, this may include a bottle-insulating compartment anyway)
- **Portable bottle-warmers** (see page 109).

Sterilisers

All your new baby's feeding equipment (including breast pumps) must be properly sterilised. Milk is a breeding ground for harmful bacteria and small babies are especially vulnerable to them. If equipment is not sterilised the bacteria can multiply swiftly; regular sterilising makes sure the equipment is a 'no-go' area for bacteria.

You don't need to buy a steriliser – bottles can be sterilised in a pan of boiling water – but if you are planning to bottle-feed your baby it can be a useful piece of equipment to have and will make your life easier.

If you are mainly breast-feeding but, say, giving your baby a bottle a day, a steriliser is still an unnecessary extra. You can always opt to buy one later if you find you are making up more bottles than you expected or if you decide to switch to bottle-feeding completely.

Types of steriliser

Apart from the boiling-water method (see box on page 107) there are three methods of sterilising: steam method, cold-water method (also known as chemical sterilisation) and microwave method. You can buy sterilisers designed specifically for each of these.

Steam sterilisers

With this type, you place your bottles upside-down in the steriliser, add water and switch it on. The water is heated electrically. When sterilisation has finished (usually after about ten minutes) the steriliser switches off automatically.

Pros:
✔ easy and quick to use
✔ minimum pre- and post-sterilisation preparation.

Cons:
✘ the most expensive type of steriliser (expect to pay around £25–40)
✘ you need to be careful not to burn your hands once sterilisation is complete – the inside of the unit can be very hot.

Cold-water sterilisers

Here, tablets or liquid containing a dilute bleach are placed into a measured amount of cold water inside the steriliser tank. Bottles must then be completely immersed in the solution, making sure there are no air bubbles where bacteria could survive (you need to be especially careful about this if the bottles are sterilised lying on their side). Sterilisation usually takes around 30 minutes. The bottles need to be rinsed in recently boiled water before use to completely get rid of the chemical solution. This type of steriliser costs around £18–20 (Boots★ and Mothercare★ both sell standard models for £18.50).

Pros:

✔ nothing to heat up so no chance of painful accidents

✔ no need for electricity or a microwave so you can use it anywhere

✔ traditional method that many hospitals use – some parents find it reassuring to stick with the way it was done while they were in hospital.

Cons:

✘ more fiddly than other methods

✘ you need to keep track of when you last changed the solution – it needs to be changed every 24 hours

✘ relatively slow sterilising process

✘ heavy to move when filled.

Microwave sterilisers

In this method you place the bottles in the steriliser with a small amount of water, fasten the lid, place it in the microwave and switch on according to the steriliser manufacturer's instructions. Sterilisation takes about ten minutes.

Pros:

✔ if you have a microwave, this is likely to be the most convenient method for you

✔ fast and simple

✔ one of the cheapest methods (this type costs £12–20).

Cons:

✘ generally these only take four bottles – other types take six or eight – so not as convenient for parents of exclusively bottle-fed new babies (or multiple births!)

✘ some sterilisers can't be used in the most powerful, modern microwaves – check before you buy

✘ some may not fit in smaller microwaves.

If you only need to sterilise one bottle, instead of using a steriliser you can buy specially designed **steriliser bottles** for microwave sterilisation (you shouldn't try to sterilise normal bottles in the microwave without the right equipment as there could be spots left that aren't properly sterile). This is a quick and simple method, especially for parents of babies who are not exclusively bottle-fed. Mothercare★ sells these bottles at £19.95 for six.

Other features to look for

- Cold-water sterilisers can be very heavy to move when filled with water, so a sturdy handle is important.
- Some sterilisers come with tongs and/or a tray to hold smaller items such as teats, so you don't have to reach too far down into the unit to retrieve them.
- Sterilisers that take both standard and wide-necked bottles are more versatile – you may find that your baby gets on better with one type of bottle, so if your steriliser only takes the 'wrong' type you could find yourself buying another.
- Larger sterilisers that take up to eight bottles at a time can be more convenient if you are doing a lot of bottle-feeding.
- Sterilisers that have space for feeding bowls and training cups will be useful during the weaning stage (babies start using these from four months or so and it is recommended that all feeding equipment should be sterilised at this age).
- Some sterilisers can be used with more than one method of sterilisation – for example, microwave and cold water. This can be useful if you need one when away from home if a microwave may not be available.
- **Travel sterilisers** are smaller than standard ones so can be handy for holidays. Generally they are designed to accommodate a couple of bottles rather than the six or so that standard sterilisers take. Some are suitable for just one method of sterilisation (e.g steam); others can be used with more than one (Boots★ sells a travel steriliser that can be used for cold-water sterilising or microwave). Alternatively, as long as a microwave is available, steriliser bottles (see previous page) or reusable steriliser bags (made by Lindam★) are easy to carry and simple to use.

The boiling-water method

If your baby has just an occasional bottle and you don't want any more baby paraphernalia taking up space in your kitchen, boiling bottles in water is a cheap and relatively quick method of sterilisation. You put the items you want sterilised into a large pan of boiling water. The water should be brought back to the boil and boiled for ten minutes before you remove the items. A disadvantage with this method, however, is that it can make rubber teats spongy and swollen – check them regularly and discard any that seem damaged.

" We used our microwave steriliser all the time – but more than that, I would say our microwave itself has been one of the most useful pieces of 'baby' equipment we've got. We rarely used it before we had Jessie, but we have used it since practically every day – first for sterilising and now for defrosting and heating her food, which I make in batches and freeze. "

Cathy, mother of Jessie, 18 months

Bottle-warmers

Using a bottle-warmer can be a convenient way of ensuring that your baby's milk is heated to the right temperature. You generally fill the warmer with water, which is then heated by an element, which in turn heats your baby's feed. Most will fit jars of baby food as well as various sizes of bottles. The length of time the feed will take to heat varies depending on the warmer, but you can generally expect a 4oz bottle of milk from the fridge to take about six minutes. A larger amount of feed will take longer and feed already at room temperature will take a shorter time to heat.

Do you need one?

Whether or not you need a bottle-warmer depends on how happy you are with using the other standard bottle-warming methods. The time-honoured method of sticking the bottle in a jug of warm water for a couple of minutes has been used by generations of parents, is a cheap and effective way of heating milk and requires no extra equipment. You will need to test the milk's temperature by shaking a few drops on to the inside of your wrist. If it's too hot, you just put it in a jug of cold water for a short time.

Many parents use the microwave to heat milk, despite the official advice being that this is not recommended because of the risk of hot spots in the milk burning your baby's mouth. A microwave is a quick and easy way of heating a bottle, but you must be absolutely sure to shake the bottle so that there are no hot spots.

If you know that you will need to heat up a lot of bottles and you want to get it right first time, every time, then a bottle-warmer could be for you. A bottle-warmer may suit those parents who don't like the idea of microwave heating or the more 'hit or miss' method of a warm jug of water. Bottle-warmers can be particularly handy for night-time feeding: as long as you get everything ready the night before, you can have the warmer next to your bed and you won't have to trudge to the kitchen to prepare the milk.

Don't automatically assume, however, that your baby will reject unheated milk. Babies don't have to have their milk warmed and some are perfectly happy with room-temperature or even cold milk. You could save yourself money and time by finding out sooner rather than later how fussy your baby is about milk temperature.

Types of bottle-warmer
There are three main types of bottle-warmer: standard, 'feeding-system' and portable.

Standard bottle-warmers
These are the most common type, and will heat up one bottle of milk (or jar of feed). You place the bottle in the central vessel of the warmer, fill around it with water from a jug, and switch it on. The water is heated by an element which in turn heats the bottle of milk. These warmers normally have an indicator light, which goes off when the milk reaches the right temperature, and a thermostat, which keeps the temperature of the water constant. Most will need de-scaling. It is useful to buy one with a timer so you know how long the milk has been in – not all warmers have these. If you think you will be using the bottle-warmer to heat jars of food as well as milk, you should choose one that has some sort of adaptor for

holding jars at an easily reachable height – otherwise you can end up reaching down into the hot warmer for your jar. Some warmers have the facility to heat food in a bowl too. Standard bottle warmers cost around £15–20.

'Feeding-system' bottle-warmers

These are more sophisticated than the standard type. They heat milk in the same way but also have a cooler section to keep a couple of filled bottles chilled and ready for warming. This could be particularly useful at night if you want to avoid having to go to the kitchen to get the milk out of the fridge (although you could simply use a standard warmer and have the filled bottle ready in a cool-bag by the bed). It's worth looking for one with added extras, such as a timer and jar holder, for instance. Feeding-system warmers cost around £30.

Portable bottle-warmers

These are the simplest type of bottle-warmer available, costing around £8–13. They are designed so you can easily warm a bottle up when you are out and about, although the milk will generally take longer to warm up than in other types of warmers, so you have to plan ahead to some extent. They work in various ways, depending on the product. Car bottle-warmers can be plugged into your car's cigarette lighter and have a webbing strap or wrap that fits around the bottle of milk or jar of baby food. (You need to plan ahead to use it otherwise you could have 15 minutes of hungry screaming.) Try children's stores; or JoJo Maman Bébé★ sells one for £7.99 which heats the contents in around 15 minutes.

Thermos produces a bottle-warmer based on the idea of a flask (available from the Boots★ website and some branches for £9.99). It is made up of two sections: an inner flask and a lid deep enough to hold a bottle. Before you go out, you fill the flask with boiling water and attach the lid. When you need to heat up the bottle of milk you remove the lid, put the bottle in it then fill around it with the hot water from the flask. The milk can take just a few minutes to heat up. The water should stay sufficiently hot enough for a few hours to warm the bottle.

> ❝We bought a bottle-warmer for night-time feeding but we have only used it a couple of times – that's because one of us usually fancies a cup of tea when Jay wakes up so it seems easier to use the boiling water from the kettle to heat the bottle instead.❞
>
> Dave, father of Jay, 6 months

Formula milk

Cows' milk isn't suitable for young babies' digestive systems, so formula milks have been developed to mimic the properties of breast milk. Like breast milk, these have the right balance of vitamins, minerals and fat for a growing baby. Most people buy their formula milk (often referred to as just 'formula') in powder form in large tubs, although you can also buy ready-mixed formula, which is useful for holidays or other times when mixing your own is inconvenient. Make sure you choose the type of formula suitable for your baby – it should be clear from the labelling on the tub which is the most appropriate.

There are three basic categories of formula milk, regardless of the brand:

- **standard** formula milk – suitable from birth or if changing from breast-feeding
- milk for **'hungrier'** bottle-fed babies – also suitable from birth but curd- rather than whey-based so has a different balance of milk proteins, which some babies find more filling
- **'follow-on'** milk, for older babies from around six months and toddlers – rich in iron and vitamins C and D, all of which are important for babies of this age and which cows' milk does not provide in adequate quantities.

Most formula milks are based on cows' milk protein, but you can buy soya-based formula if your baby shows an intolerance to standard formula – talk to your GP or health visitor first if you think your baby is having problems digesting the formula you are using.

"Connor always wanted warm milk when we were out for the afternoon. I never bothered with a portable warmer. Before we left, I used to put boiling water in his bottle and put the required amount of powered milk in a lidded plastic beaker. When he wanted his milk, which was usually an hour or so after we went out, I just used to mix the two together. It was always warm enough for him."

Jan, mother of Connor, 19 months

"It wasn't until Esther was about three months old that I discovered ready-mixed formula – I wish someone had told me about it before. I keep a couple of the small cartons in my bag so I know I'll always have some milk at hand and I don't have to think about making it up before we go out."

Dawn, mother of Esther, 6 months

Breast-feeding accessories

Breast-feeding is one of the most natural human functions so, arguably, there should be no need to kit yourself out with breast-feeding accessories – your breasts and your baby should do just fine together. Suffice to say, however, manufacturers have other ideas and have developed a wide range of breast-feeding products designed to help you out. To be fair, some can indeed be quite handy. Whether or not they will be useful to you depends very much on factors such as how easy you find breast-feeding, how discreet you want to be when feeding your baby and what you want your baby to be fed on when you're at work or away.

Breast pumps

With a bit of practice you can express your own milk, so theoretically there should be no need to buy a breast pump. Having said that, some women find expressing their own milk difficult or they simply don't want to do it, and this is when a breast pump can be extremely useful. They are effective not just at enabling you to express milk to give to your baby in a bottle or to store in the freezer for later, but at relieving the breast discomfort that can occur when, for example, your baby misses a feed but your breasts are still producing the same amount of milk.

There are three main types of breast pump.

- **Large electric pumps** – These are the most effective. Used by hospitals, they are not widely available to buy but you may be able to hire one for a monthly fee from your local National Childbirth Trust (NCT)★ or La Leche League★ breast-feeding counsellor. If you will need to express daily at home – say, if you are going to work and need milk supplies ready for the next day – it is worth considering hiring one. The main disadvantage of these pumps is that they are quite bulky pieces of equipment and not at all portable, so they won't suit everyone.
- **Manual pumps** – These work by hand-operated pump action. They are the simplest type of pump and the cheapest (costing around £25). They are light to carry around so are especially useful if you need to express while you are out or at work. They do, however, requite a bit of a knack to operate them effectively and your hand may get tired of pumping after a while.
- **Battery/mains powered pumps** – These are versatile because you can choose which power source to use. They don't involve much effort, as you simply position the pump and switch on. They can be more expensive than the manual sort (they cost £20–45) and are not as discreet as they make a slight noise when in use.

Many women who buy breast pumps have high expectations of them that aren't fulfilled. A common complaint is that using them involves a lot of effort or inconvenience for very little gain. Getting used to them can take a bit of practice, and if you give up altogether after numerous half-hours spent expressing little more than a mouthful of milk, no one can blame you for not trying. A breast pump that works very well for one person may not work nearly as well for the next. But if you find a pump that works for you, it can become an indispensable part of your breast-feeding regime. If you can, try to borrow a couple of different types from friends so that you can have a few trial runs before you buy. (Bear in mind that your milk supply may be variable; that if on some days you can express more than on others this is not necessarily related to the pump.)

❝I tried all the types of breast pump. I used a large electric one in hospital when my first baby was in special care, but I really didn't want to hire such a cumbersome thing to use at home. Next was a small battery type, but I found this a bit fiddly and not very effective. I tried hand expressing, but to be honest I never felt comfortable 'milking' myself in such an obvious way. The hand pump-action type I got on with a lot better – as long as you positioned it properly it seemed to work really well.❞

Roisin, mother of Samuel, age 2, and Kali, 6 months

❝If you have a battery/mains operated pump, make sure you only use the batteries when you really have to as I found they run low pretty quickly. Use the adaptor to plug it into the mains instead.❞

Janine, mother of Katy, 5 months

Storing your milk

Breast-milk freezer bags are widely available and are handy for storage. They have a measurement scale printed on them so you know how much milk they contain.

Nursing bras

A nursing bra helps you breast-feed with minimal fuss. They look much like ordinary bras but, depending on the style, are designed to let you drop, unzip or unclip the cups so that you can feed your baby without having to hitch up or prise open the whole bra. They also tend to have wider straps, sides and back in order to provide you with adequate support. Of the three types – drop-cup, zip-cup and front-opening – drop-cup are the most widely available. All require an element of practice to undo and do up without too much fiddling. Ideally you need to get the bra properly fitted before you decide which one to buy, as your breast size will have changed from your pre-pregnancy days.

Sleep bras are designed to support your breasts at night-time. These can also be useful for keeping breast pads (see overleaf) in place while you are in bed.

Nursing tops

Special breast-feeding tops are not essential but some companies do sell them and some women may find them useful, especially during the early days when they are getting used to breast-feeding and may want to do it as discreetly as possible. These tops normally have subtle 'flaps' and a zip or poppers across the front, which you lift up or undo and then put your baby to the breast. Your breast will be fairly well covered and your baby feeds through the opening in the top. Try JoJo Maman Bébé★ or Blooming Marvellous★ for a selection of nursing tops.

There is no need for special nursing nightwear – you just need something loose-fitting with fasteners at the front that you can undo easily.

Breast pads and shells

Breasts often leak during the early breast-feeding weeks, but you can protect your clothing by using breast pads. You put these inside your bra and they absorb the milk that leaks from your nipples. You can buy packs of disposable pads or ones that you wash and reuse. The reusable ones are better value for money in the long run (and these days you can get rather nice organic silk ones), but may be less convenient if you need to replace the pads regularly. Plastic-backed pads prevent your milk from leaking right through, although they should not be necessary unless ordinary pads don't provide you with enough protection. The plastic-backed sort can also encourage sore nipples unless changed regularly. Thin wads of tissue paper inside your bra should be adequate for absorbing milk if you run out of pads or regard them as an unnecessary extra.

Breast shells have a slightly different purpose. Sometimes when you are breast-feeding, the breast your baby *isn't* feeding from can leak quite a lot. You can put a breast shell over this breast to gather the milk and store it for future bottle-feeding.

Feeding pillows

Many women like to breast- or bottle-feed with their baby resting on a pillow on their lap. You can buy specially shaped pillows that can make feeding even more comfortable (although any reasonably firm, standard bed pillow can work well). Alternatively, you can use the pillow yourself to support your back while you are breast-feeding (or during pregnancy or labour). Feeding pillows come in two basic styles – either V-shaped or gently curved. Both styles can make feeding more comfortable, although the V-shaped style can also be useful as a back support (you may find these being marketed as all-round 'support' pillows rather than specifically as feeding pillows).

Many mothers swear by these pillows, which are widely available from department or nursery stores and usually cost around £20–25. The pillows normally have a foam, feather or bean-bag core. Bear in mind it may be worth buying a spare cover if available, as the pillows can easily become stained with milk.

Breast pain relief

There are times when your breasts can be very uncomfortable after you have given birth and during breast-feeding. Sore, cracked nipples is one temporary but unfortunate possible side-effect of breast-feeding. Soothing nipple creams, designed to help alleviate this, are available – a well-known brand is Kamillosan chamomile ointment (which can also double-up as a mild nappy-rash cream). Alternatively, midwives and health visitors often suggest gently rubbing expressed breast milk into the affected part.

Pain from engorged breasts – for example, when your milk first starts coming in or when you are producing more milk than your baby is taking – is very common. Vinyl breast packs are available to help (for example, Breast Nurse from Mothercare*, at £12.50 for two). These are filled with a gel and can be cooled in the fridge or warmed in a pan of hot water before being placed inside your bra.

> **"**I bought a V-shaped support pillow while I was pregnant. I used it before I had Danny and afterwards for breast-feeding as it was the only way I could do it comfortably. It made feeding in hospital easier (although they told me to keep an eye on it as they sometimes 'went missing', such was their desirability in the maternity ward!). Later it became a support for Danny while he was learning to sit. I passed it on to my friend when she was pregnant and she has had just as much use out of it. **"**
>
> Claire, mother of Danny, age 2

The best overall 'cure' for painful breasts and nipples, however, is to persist in trying to establish a comfortable breast-feeding routine.

Baby food and drink

The official guidance is that you shouldn't start your baby on solid food until he or she is six months old, although many parents are happy to start weaning some time between four and six months. Before this age, babies' delicate digestive systems aren't fully developed enough to cope easily with anything other than milk or water. Most parents start off by giving their babies baby rice, which you buy in packets and mix with boiled water or milk. Baby rice is very bland, so your baby gets used to the texture of food before experiencing any real taste. Formula or breast milk should still be the main source of nourishment. By the time your baby is about six months old, as long as everything is mashed up or puréed, his or her taste buds and stomach are more or less ready for most of the foods you eat.

Shop-bought or home-made?

The big question faced by most parents once they start proper weaning is whether to go for shop-bought packets and jars of food, to make home-made baby food, or to do a bit of both. Manufactured baby foods have clear advantages in terms of convenience. You don't have to do any scraping, boiling or puréeing – you just pop open the jar and down it goes (with some babies, without any need for heating up either). If you feed straight from the jar, you don't even have to do any washing-up.

For many parents, however, this kind of convenience isn't the be-all and end-all. Home-made food also has clear advantages, not least because you have control over exactly what your baby eats. You know where the food comes from and that it doesn't contain any ingredients you don't know about. You can alter the texture of the food and experiment with different tastes and mixtures to suit your baby's progress (use either a special blender for baby food or a hand-held blender; or you can mash soft food up with a fork). Home-made meals can be cheaper if you're using the same foods that the rest of the family is eating, and can also help babies get used to the taste of home-prepared food. Neither does home-made food need to be much less convenient – you can, for example, make batches of food to freeze in ice-cube trays and defrost small amounts when you need it.

But whatever your intentions, it is fairly likely that you will buy at least some manufactured baby food, even if only to keep in the cupboard for an emergency or for travelling. So how do you choose between the large number of brands and types available?

Types of baby food

Manufactured baby meals come in two main types: 'wet', pre-cooked meals, mostly in jars and cans; and dry foods in packs (these have to be mixed with water or milk). Frozen baby meals are also available. The meals are labelled or categorised depending on what age of baby they are aimed at. Within these you can choose between the increasingly popular organic ranges or non-organic types. Then you have a choice from a vast range of flavours and recipes – from 'turkey dinner' and 'apple pie dessert' to chicken korma and cour-gette risotto with banana.

Looking at the labels

Beyond making sure that the meal is the right one for your baby's age, what you opt for is a matter of your own and your baby's pref-erences. What many parents may fail to do, however, is to look at the ingredients on the jar or packet. If you do study these, what you see may well influence your choice.

Sugar alert

Government recommendations are that baby foods should usually be free from, or low in, sugars, including those from fruit juice. Nevertheless, many of the baby foods available contain sugar, fruit juice or both. Breakfast meals are likely to contain sugar, some 'savoury' meals contain glucose syrup, a form of sugar, and many desserts contain some form of added sugar. Sucrose, glucose, dextrose, glucose syrup, honey, fruit juice concentrates and fruit syrups are all types of sugar to look out for on the label.

More starch than food

Other ingredients in baby foods that can give cause for concern are additives such as starches, gums and maltodextrin, which are used by some manufacturers to thicken and alter the texture of food. Critics feel that because starches absorb water these can 'pad out' the meal so there's less 'real' food in it. Some brands clearly state that they don't add starches, while others contain more starch than the ingredients featured in the name of the product. Check the label for starch content if you want more food for your money.

Other ingredients with health implications

- Babies under six months old should avoid wheat-based cereals because these contain the protein **gluten**, which can cause a reaction in some people. Some food for babies under six months is not gluten-free. However, the presence of gluten as an ingredient has to be stated on the label, so check this if you are concerned.
- **Salty** food should not be eaten by babies, and the amount of salt that manufacturers can add to baby food is regulated.
- **Pesticide residues** can be present in many foods but the law now requires that all baby food meets stricter limits on pesticides, and some pesticides will be banned from crops used in baby food.
- It is still not known whether BSE could have passed to sheep. There are controls to remove what would be the most infective parts of the animal in case BSE should be present, but these would not remove most of the infectivity from **lamb**. Consumers' Association (CA) has called on the Food Standards Agency (FSA)★ to offer guidance on the issue, so that parents can make an informed choice about the lamb used in baby food. CA has also pushed for baby-food manufacturers to state which country the lamb comes from. For more information, see the FSA website.

Comparing brands

Different brands and ranges of baby food will contain different proportions of ingredients and different levels of starch and sugar. Try to get into the practice of looking at the labels to see what kinds of ingredients baby meals contain. Ingredients are listed in order of weight, with the biggest first. If the ingredient appears in the name of the food, the percentage must be stated, but for other ingredients the exact percentage does not have to be labelled – so it is this order that is the key to how much sugar, starch, etc. is in a product. Added sugars and fruit juices can encourage a sweet tooth, and water, as well as starch, may be used to 'pad out' a meal.

Meaningless labels

Some manufacturers exploit the worries that many parents have about the foods they are giving their children by making claims on the label that, although true, have little or no useful meaning. Treat with a pinch of salt baby-food labels that make the following claims.

- **'No artificial flavourings'** – official recommendations are that baby foods are flavoured only with natural foods, or food extracts and oils.
- **'No artificial colours'** – these are banned in baby food anyway.
- **'No added salt'** – The amount of salt that can be added to baby food is controlled by law.
- **'No added sugar'** – This doesn't mean no added fruit juice.
- **'No preservatives'** – Preservatives are not allowed in baby food (although some antioxidants, such as vitamin C, are added to stop food going off).

Baby-food scares

You naturally want your baby's food to be pure and safe to eat. But scares over the content of shop-bought baby food seem to hit the headlines every few years. A recent controversy (in 2003) has been over the substance semicarbazide. This is a chemical that forms during the manufacture of the plastic seal used in the metal lids of glass jars. Scientists carrying out routine safety checks found that semicarbazide was somehow leaking into food in jars. Although the levels found were extremely small, some of the highest concentrations were found in baby foods – probably because the jars are small and the ratio of seal to food is higher than for other foods. Semicarbazide has been found to be a cancer-causing substance in some animal studies. The Food Standards Agency (FSA)* says that parents shouldn't stop buying food in jars, because any risk of harm is minimal. However, manufacturers have been asked to look into ways of reducing the risk of the chemical getting into baby foods by developing new types of lids. The FSA website provides advice on how you can prepare your own baby food if you have concerns.

Drinks

Milk and water are the best drinks for your baby or toddler, but it's not very realistic or practical to expect parents to stick to these and these alone. Small children like fruit juice and it can provide them with important vitamins. Fruit juice does contain naturally present sugar, however, so it is advisable to water the juice down. Some fruit drinks are marketed specifically for babies and are usually some sort of non-acidic fruit juice, such as apple, mixed with water – Cow & Gate, for example, produces such a range.

Although products such as these may be handy for travelling, it is far cheaper to simply water down your own cartons of juice and give this to your baby in a cup (juice in bottles is not recommended as it can encourage tooth decay).

Highchairs

A highchair of one form or another is one of the few essentials for an older baby. They are not suitable for use until your baby can sit unsupported (usually at around six to nine months) – although you can buy highchairs that are adaptable for young babies, before the six-month stage many parents use a bouncy cradle or other type of baby chair at feeding time (for more on these see pages 43–6).

Once the time is right for a highchair, though, you and your baby will appreciate the benefits. You won't have to crouch down for feeding and he or she will feel part of the family sitting at table-height to eat meals. As long as your baby is strapped in, a highchair will provide a safe eating place and a prime viewing position for him or her to watch you busying about the kitchen or eating your food. You can also use the highchair as a play chair, by placing toys or kitchen utensils on the tray and letting your baby entertain him- or herself as you get on with other things. Some types of highchairs convert to chairs that toddlers and even older children can use.

What to look for in a highchair
There are numerous types of highchair on the market but, whichever sort you pick, you should look out for certain qualities before you make your choice.

- Is the seat reasonably padded and comfortable-looking? Your baby will be using the highchair a lot and anything that helps to make him or her want to stay in the chair rather than squirm out will be of benefit. Likewise a larger seat is better than a smaller one.

- Is the seat wipe-clean? A fabric cover that you can remove and put in the washing machine just isn't practical enough. You need to have a seat you can wipe after every feed.

- Does the chair fold easily and neatly? Not all highchairs fold up but if you want one that does, you should be able to fold and store it with minimal effort – otherwise it's bound to remain standing as a semi-permanent kitchen fixture. Models that stand when folded, rather than needing to be leaned against a wall, can be useful if the chair is to remain in the kitchen rather than be stored away (although these can take up more space). With some highchairs you have to remove the tray before you fold it – this is an added burden if you plan to put it away regularly. Try out a selection of folding highchairs in the shop.

- How big is the tray? As a general rule, the bigger the tray the better. Think of the tray as needing to be roomy enough to hold a selection of playthings rather than simply a bowl or a cup.

- Does the tray look easy to keep clean? Bear in mind that both wooden and plastic trays can stain – although varnished wood tends to be less likely to stain. Indentations in the tray, such as a dip for holding a cup, are a nuisance rather than a good design feature because they make cleaning more difficult. Likewise, angular ridges on the edge of the tray simply become food traps. A high, curved rim is best.

- Can you detach the tray? A detachable tray is a useful feature if you would like the option of your baby sitting right up to the main table (although the design of some tables may not allow you to push the highchair close enough). It will also make cleaning easier. Check that the tray is simple to detach, however, otherwise you may not bother. Alternatively, a flip-over tray will also enable your baby to feed at the table.

- Can you adjust the tray? Adjustable trays give your baby more room as he or she grows. If you like the look of a highchair with a fixed tray, look at the gap between the tray and the chair and think about squeezing a chubby toddler in there – some chairs with fixed trays have quite a narrow gap. Others are positioned too far away for some babies to reach their food comfortably.

- Does the harness have shoulder straps? A lap belt alone is neither supportive nor secure and babies can slip. A five-point harness – where retention straps fix to five points on the chair – gives much better security and upper back support than three-point systems. Without shoulder straps, determined older children can stand up in the seat. A crotch strap or bar should also be present to stop the child sliding out.
- Are there any uncomfortable edges? Feel under the tray and around the edge of the seat area for sharp rims. You don't want to be scraping your toddler's thighs every time you lift him or her in or out of the chair.
- If there are integral straps, can these be removed? The straps often end up being the most food-encrusted bit of the highchair, and it is useful to be able to wash them properly.
- If the chair has height/seat/tray-position adjustments, are these simple and quick to do? If not, you may well not bother using them. Try out a range of adjustments in the shop.

Types of highchair

There are five main types of highchair available. All have their advantages and disadvantages.

Standard highchairs

These are the simplest type of traditional-looking highchair and have one height position. You can buy fold-up versions and models with useful extra features, such as a detachable tray. Expect to pay around £30–40 for a simple, standard highchair.

Pros:

✔ generally the cheapest type, apart from travel highchairs (see page 125)
✔ one height is adequate for most people
✔ tend to be lighter and fold flatter than other types.

Cons:

✘ lack of seat-height adjustability means they're less versatile
✘ not all will have other useful features like an adjustable or detachable tray.

Multi-position highchairs

With these you can adjust the seat height so that you feed your baby at a low or high level. Many have five or six adjustable height positions. On some models you can also adjust the seat so it reclines. Most can be folded and many have extras such as varied-position trays. Expect to pay between £40 and £110 for this type of chair.

Pros:

✔ height adjustability means you can feed your baby at a position that suits you best – self-feeding toddlers may prefer the low level, for example, or you can use this level for a smaller baby if you prefer to feed him or her lower down

✔ models with reclining seats can be used for newborn babies and to bottle-feed, so extend the lifespan of the highchair

✔ depending on the model, they are not necessarily much more expensive than the standard type.

Cons:

✘ the adjustments may not be particularly easy to make – many parents find one position they are happy with and stick with it, so the height-adjustment element may be a bit redundant

✘ some models can be quite heavy and cumbersome to move – also they are fairly large so aren't a good choice if you're short on space.

Convertible highchairs

Often referred to as 'three-in-one' combinations, these can be used as a highchair for younger babies then converted into a toddler-sized chair and matching low table when your child reaches the self-feeding stage. They are usually made of wood. On some models the wooden seat has a padded cover, but if there isn't one built in you should be able to buy one separately. This sort of chair costs between £40 and £100.

Pros:

✔ toddlers who protest at being put into their highchair, whether in a high or low position, may feel more grown-up (and eat more happily) with their own chair and table

✔ style-wise, at least, the wood design can be more acceptable to many parents as a piece of kitchen furniture

✔ once you have finished using the chair and table in the kitchen, they can go into your child's bedroom as an extra piece of furniture (larger models can be used for children up to the age of 5).

Cons:

✘ cube chairs can't be folded and so take up permanent space in your kitchen

✘ if you have your second child soon after your first, you're unlikely to get the best use out of the chair because you'll want to use it as a highchair again before your elder child has had full use of it as a chair and table

✘ less likely to have the 'added extras' of some other highchairs, such as recline positions and an easily removable tray

✘ some models are cumbersome to assemble – try before you buy if possible.

Baby-to-adult highchairs

Unusual-looking but innovatively designed, these are a type of highchair that can be adjusted for use by all ages. There are three main brands available in the UK – the Tripp Trapp (by Stokke★), the MultiSitt (available from Cheeky Rascals★ and Green Baby★) and the Babydan highchair (available from Mothercare★). All have a broadly similar design. A long, slanting wooden back is interspersed with slats or slots into which you position a wooden seat, footrest and safety bar. Where you position them depends on how big your child is. Your baby will normally sit, secured with a safety bar and a harness, at the table (although with the MultiSitt you can buy a separate tray). When your child gets older you remove the safety bar and adjust the height of the seat appropriately. An adult would be able to use this as an occasional chair with the seat at a low position. Expect to pay £100 or so, plus extra for attachments such as a tray.

Pros:

✔ a versatile seat that can 'grow' with your child

✔ designed so your child can always sit at the correct height at the table

✔ fits in well with other modern-looking dining and kitchen furniture

✔ no need to buy a booster seat (see 'Travel or portable highchairs', below) or other children's chairs or tables when your child gets older.

Cons:

✘ more expensive than most other highchairs

✘ can be heavy so not very manoeuvrable

✘ with a second child, you may find yourself buying a standard highchair anyway, as the idea is that your first child should still be using the seat. Alternatively, you may decide to spend another £100 on another of the same seats, and so on with any subsequent children – and you could end up feeling that you have bought yourself a lifestyle rather than a highchair.

Travel or portable highchairs

A travel or portable highchair can be used instead of a conventional highchair at any time. Both types – table seat or folding booster seat – can be used from age six months or so, are cheap, save on space and can be taken with you when you go away. Suffice to say, they don't have the added extras of other types of highchair, but you may not want these anyway. Expect to pay £10–50 depending on the type. For more about travel highchairs see pages 156–9.

An innovative new type of baby seat is the Bumbo baby-sitter. The seat is made from plastic and specially moulded so that your baby's own body weight holds him or her in the chair. It is suitable for babies from four to twelve months and, although not a highchair, it can be useful for feeding younger babies because it has a wipe-clean surface (unlike bouncy cradles, which are the other feeding-chair option – see pages 43–6). It is also more portable than a highchair. Mothercare★ sells the Bumbo baby-sitter for £27.95.

A panel of families tried out the Bumbo for *Which?* in August 2003. All said it was robust and easy to clean, but there were mixed feelings about its usefulness. The overall verdict was that if you want one, you need to time your purchase carefully because to use the Bumbo your baby needs to be strong enough to sit upright yet at the same time not able to pull his or her legs free or tip the seat over. In addition, if your baby has particularly plump thighs, the seat may not be comfortable.

Second-hand highchairs

Highchairs are often used second-hand. If you do buy a second-hand one or use a hand-me-down, check that:

- it is stable, sturdy and isn't missing any screws or bolts
- it has an integral harness; if it hasn't, buy a separate harness and use it every time your baby is in the chair
- there are no sharp edges or elements such as cracks or breaks on the plastic tray that could pinch your child
- no foam is exposed on the seat – babies could pick it out and choke on it.

Which? Best Buy highchairs

Which? tested highchairs in January 2004. Parents tried out standing chairs at home and a nursery also used them for a month.

Safety watch

Parents clearly want to feel confident that the highchair they buy isn't going to topple over with their child in it. But, surprisingly, there are no legal safety requirements specific to highchairs. Many manufacturers claim compliance with British Standard 5799 but this standard is non-compulsory and child safety experts agree that the 17-year-old standard is outdated. Despite much campaigning and discussion, participating countries were, at the time of writing, unable to agree a new joint European standard.

The stability of a highchair could be a particular concern if the highchair can be positioned next to a table and your baby is able to push backwards against the table with his or her feet. In 2003, Which? carried out some stability tests on the Tripp Trapp chair (see page 124) after an incident in which a baby rocked the chair by pushing her feet against the table so that the chair overturned with her in it. The Tripp Trapp passed the tests – but only just. In addition, in January 2004 Which? tested a selection of highchairs for stability (as well as strength and general safety) using the existing British Standard as the benchmark. These tests showed no serious safety concerns. However, tougher extra tests to assess the stability of the highchairs when they were pushed backwards

Portable travel chairs were also tested and taken out and about by the parents. All the chairs were also ergonomically assessed by staff in the *Which?* laboratories. Of the standard, lightweight folding chairs tested, the Bruin Patchwork Farm 270-03 (£25 from Babies 'R' Us'*) proved the Best Buy. The chair was excellent value, could be folded and unfolded easily, was easy to clean and had the safety bonus of an incorporated five-point safety harness. However, it doesn't have an adjustable tray. The Best Buy in the convertible/three-in-one category was the Nazca chair from Jané* (£90), mainly available from independent nursery stores. This was easy to assemble, the tray easy to clean and adjustable, and the chair has a comfortable padded seat. The main drawback was the three-point rather than five-point harness. The Chicco Hippo Table Seat (£35), was the Best Buy for portable chairs. It was easy to attach to the table and very secure, though quite tricky to keep clean as food got trapped in the crevices and seams of the fabric. The Chicco

revealed that two chairs could be overturned more easily than should be the case. Which? has suggested to the British Standards Institution (the body responsible for safety standards) that a more rigorous standard is overdue and that any new standard should assess how the floor the high-chair stands on and nearby tables affect stability.

Whatever the ins and outs of current safety standards, the golden rules for highchair safety at home are:

- *Never leave your baby unattended in a highchair.*
- *Secure your baby in the highchair at all times with a safety harness – either the integral one supplied or a separate one complying with British Standard 6684. Attach the harness as soon as your child is seated.*
- *Be careful lifting your child in and out of the highchair (if your baby is struggling or catches his or her foot under the tray the whole highchair could fall over).*
- *Do not use a highchair on a slippery, raised or uneven surface.*
- *Store the highchair out of your child's reach when folded.*
- *if you have to do something else away from your baby, make sure the highchair is positioned away from anything within your baby's reach.*

Mamma Highchair (with highchair toy, £110) was the Best Buy in the multi-function category. Roomy and luxurious feeling, it folded up easily and compactly. The tray, however, was judged to be a little high for smaller babies. The Chicco range is available from John Lewis*.

Highchair accessories

There are toys designed specifically to be used on a highchair (although bear in mind that your baby may get just as much entertainment from a wooden spoon and a plastic box). The main advantage with highchair toys is that you can attach them to the highchair, either with a suction pad or tied to the frame, so you won't be constantly stooping to pick up the toy once your baby has discovered the joys of throwing things on the floor. The drawback is, of course, that he or she will get bored with seeing the same old highchair toy every day, so try to vary the toys if you want to get maximum benefit. You can find a range of toys suitable for highchairs at children's stores.

Another potentially useful accessory is a plastic mat that you can place under the highchair to catch all the spills. This is especially handy if you have a floor that is a nuisance to clean. Make sure the mat covers a reasonable area around the highchair, as spills won't necessarily be falling directly underneath. Mats are widely available from children's stores. Alternatively, you can spread newspaper on the floor.

> **"** Our first child got mostly hand-me-downs, including his highchair, so with our second we felt we should get her something new. We chose a simple cube highchair from Mothercare and it has been really versatile. Alice currently uses it in all its different forms. She has it in its highchair position at the table, as a low chair with its tray for snacks or for playing and as a table for things like drawing. We use a separate chair when she has it as a table as the tray is a hassle to take on and off but otherwise it is easy to adjust once you know how. The tray is especially good as it is large and quite deep. Alice even uses it for water play. **"**
>
> Teresa, mother of Alice, 2 and Jesse, 4

Bibs

By the time your baby reaches the weaning stage, you are already likely to be feeling that the cycle of clothes-washing is playing a rather dominant role in your life. Anything that helps to keep that pile of soiled and smelly baby garments to a minimum is a piece of equipment worth having. The bib is a trusty stalwart of babyhood which has saved many a garment from the wash cycle until absolutely necessary. Many parents with babies who posset or dribble a lot are likely to have been using bibs regularly from the early days, but it's when the likes of puréed carrot and strawberry fromage frais start to appear on the scene that the true value of a decent bib is evident.

Types of bib

You will probably be surprised at the range of different types of bib available. You can, of course, buy the traditional semi-circle of towelling with ties for the neck, but you could also choose pull-on bibs, long-sleeved cover-all 'super' bibs, rigid plastic bibs with in-built 'crumb' trays, disposable bibs and more. All will protect your baby's clothes and so perform basically the same job, but there are differences between the various types.

With all bibs, as long as they don't get in the way or are uncomfortable to wear, it's a case of the bigger the better once your baby gets into the idea of feeding him- or herself. You don't have to buy bibs, however. A muslin cloth tied at the neck will cover your baby very well and washes easily. In fact, any easily washable fabric can become a make-shift bib, especially during early weaning. It's when your baby gets a bit older and more coordinated in terms of pulling off whatever you put on him or her that you may appreciate a manufactured bib with child-proof fastenings.

Traditional towelling bibs

You can buy small versions of these for young babies, to help protect clothes from possetting, milk spills or dribbling, or you can buy larger versions for when your baby starts to eat. You usually attach them with ties or a Velcro fastening, or they have a stretch head-hole that you pull over your baby's head.

Pros:

✔ simple and inexpensive (often available in multi-packs)

✔ highly absorbent

✔ some have a waterproof plastic backing to prevent liquids from soaking through – a good choice if your baby is a dribbler

✔ easy to fold up and carry around with you when you go out.

Cons:

✘ baby foods can easily stain them even if you wash them at high temperatures, so don't expect them to stay looking new for long (although brightly coloured ones may hide the stains better than pastel-coloured ones)

✘ waterproof-backed ones cannot normally be washed at the same high temperatures as all-towelling versions

✘ some are too small for an older baby, especially when he or she starts to self-feed.

Plastic scoop bibs

These have an in-built curved 'catch' tray at the base of the bib so food falls into the tray rather than into your baby's lap. They usually have adjustable hole and popper neck fastenings.

Pros:

✔ wipe-clean; some can also be put in the dishwasher

✔ good for babies trying to self-feed.

Cons:

✘ rigid plastic versions can be stiff and uncomfortable around the neck – look for those with a soft neck rim or ones made from flexible rather than stiff plastic

✘ older babies may enjoy tipping everything out of the scoop tray

✘ larger scoop bibs may catch on the highchair tray and prove awkward to use.

Cover-all bibs

Usually made from plastic-coated fabric or flexible PVC, these bibs are designed to provide maximum protection for toddlers in particular. As well as covering the front, some versions have full sleeves while others cover the shoulders and upper arms. They are generally fastened with ties or Velcro.

Pros:
- ✔ best for top-to-toe protection
- ✔ can be used as protection for painting and other messy activities as well as feeding
- ✔ often have bright, fun designs that appeal to toddlers
- ✔ easy to clean.

Cons:
- ✘ some children dislike being 'dressed up' to eat and may protest
- ✘ full-arm versions sometimes have uncomfortable elasticated wrists – check for potential discomfort before you buy
- ✘ depending on the brand, can be relatively expensive.

Disposable bibs

Throw-away bibs are usually made from strengthened paper. You normally buy them in boxes of 20 and they will often have a waterproof backing as well as an absorbent front. Adhesive tapes attach the bib to the baby's clothes, although some brands have neck ties.

Pros:
- ✔ great for holidays when you don't want extra washing
- ✔ useful to keep as an 'emergency' bib in the car or changing bag or just to have on you when you're out and about
- ✔ handy for wiping everything up once your baby has finished eating.

Cons:
- ✘ can be expensive if you use them on a daily basis (Boots' disposables are £2.85 for a pack of 20 and there are other brands that cost more) – although you don't have to use a new one every time
- ✘ relatively easy for your baby to pull off.

Bowls, spoons and trainer cups

Although you can use bowls and small spoons that you already have in the house, those specifically designed for weaning do have advantages.

Bowls

Plastic bowls with high sides and a 'lip' or gripper on the edge for you to hold are convenient for when you are feeding your baby. It is useful to have a lip to grip hold of, not least because your baby is bound to try to swipe the bowl out of your hand at some stage. Once your baby is trying to self-feed, bowls with lower, gently curving sides and a textured easy-to-grip rim all round the edge can help him or her keep control (Babies 'R' Us★ has a good-value range from £2.99). 'High-tech' versions of feeding bowls include those with a compartment in the base into which you put hot water to keep the food warm; heat-sensitive bowls and spoons, which change colour when the food is cool enough to eat; and bowls with a suction base, which helps prevent spillages. Some parents find these innovations useful although they are certainly not a necessity and can make the process of feeding more complex than it needs to be. Bowls with fun designs on the base may seem gimmicky but some children like to get to the bottom of their food to see the picture, so they can be a useful feeding aid.

Spoons

Standard teaspoons are often too deep for babies to get a decent mouthful from. Shallow spoons made from flexible plastic will help a young baby to feed and are also popular as a teething accessory with some babies (Heinz produces a widely available range of soft baby spoons). Self-feeding babies and toddlers will need a deeper spoon with an easy-to-grip handle. As with feeding bowls, you can buy 'high-tech' versions of spoons: for example, Little Green Earthlets★ sells 'Munchtime White Hot Airplane' spoons which are shaped like an aeroplane and turn white if the food is too hot. Tommee Tippee also produces a heat-sensor spoon which is widely available from nursery stores and chemists.

Trainer cups

Moving from a bottle to a cup is one of those little developmental landmarks that parents often feel proud their baby has reached. You may already have a cup spout attachment for your baby's bottle if you use a 'feeding system', such as those sold in the Avent range (see 'Bottles and teats', pages 98–103). These spouts are soft and pliable and can be a useful first cup experience. Alternatively, any of the 'first' cups on the market are suitable – again, it's just a case of finding one that you and your child like.

Handles

Easily grippable handles are a big plus, especially when your baby is first starting to use a cup, because he or she will find it easy to control. The drawback is that handles also make it easier for your baby to wave the cup about – not a problem if you have a leak-proof cup (see below) but messy if you haven't. Many parents find that their babies are happy with smooth-sided beakers from an early age, and stick with these. It's a case of trying out a few types to see which is best for you.

Spouts

When your baby is first starting to use a cup, a small cup with a soft plastic spout is ideal as a transition from a bottle to a cup (Heinz makes a decent one). Once your baby has got used to the idea of a cup, there are various types you can try. The simplest are those with a basic lid and a spout. These are widely used, but don't expect this type of cup to keep leaks and spills completely at bay. As long as it is kept upright it will be fine, but once tipped sideways it will leak.

Many parents prefer the security of a leak-proof cup. These usually have a self-sealing valve so that the drink is sealed in after each sip. However, younger children may not get on with them, simply because they may have to suck quite hard to get the drink out. The valve can also wear out over time and you'll need to replace the lid. In addition, some of these cups have lids that are quite hard to get off for filling and washing. Despite these drawbacks they are highly popular, particularly the Anyway Up brand, which is widely available.

A compromise is a 'travelling' cup, with a spout that you can lift up when your child wants to drink and put down when he or she has finished. Your child can suck normally to get the drink out. The lids to these are often screw-on, so are easy to remove but don't come off when the cup is thrown on the floor. However, this sort of cup may not be completely leak-proof if it gets jiggled around a lot in your bag or in the car, as it is still possible for juice to leak through the spout when it is down.

Once your child can use a straw it isn't such a problem if you are out and about and have forgotten his or her cup – you can simply buy a mini-carton of juice. However, a juice carton can be something of a liability: small children invariably squeeze the carton too hard and juice goes flying everywhere. An innovative product to prevent this is a juice box holder: you place the carton in the box and your child holds this instead of the carton (available from Babies 'R' Us★ for £1.99). Of course, you do have to remember to take the juice box out with you instead of the cup . . .

> "One of the most useful feeding items I bought was a set of three little lidded weaning bowls from Mothercare. They were quite small and simple with a jutting-out section on the edge for you to hold. I used them for my children's first mashed-up food at home then later used them to take out snacks like chopped-up bits of fruit and raisins. They've always been really handy – in fact, I still use them and my children are now 4 and 6."

Joanne, mother of Charlie and Grace

Websites	
Babies 'R' Us	www.babiesrus.co.uk
Blooming Marvellous	www.bloomingmarvellous.co.uk
Boots	www.boots.com
Cheeky Rascals	www.cheekyrascals.co.uk
Food Standards Agency	www.food.gov.uk
Green Baby	www.greenbabyco.com
Jané	www.jane.es (worldwide)
	www.johnstonprams.co.uk (UK)
John Lewis	www.johnlewis.com
JoJo Maman Bébé	www.jojomamanbebe.co.uk
La Leche League	www.laleche.org.uk
Lindam	www.lindam.com
Little Green Earthlets	www.earthlets.co.uk
Mothercare	www.mothercare.co.uk
National Childbirth Trust	www.nct-online.org
Stokke	www.stokke.com

Feeding equipment checklist

Item	Notes
Bottles & teats	
Steriliser	
Formula milk	
Bottle-warmers	
Dishwasher basket	
Bottle-drying rack	
Bottle cooler bags	
Breast pump	
Nursing bras	
Nursing tops	
Breast pads and shells	
Feeding pillow	
Breast pain relief	
Highchair	
Highchair accessories	
Bibs	
Bowls	
Spoons	
Trainer cups	
Other	

Chapter 5

Travelling with your baby

Once you have a baby, getting from A to B safely, comfortably and as easily as possible demands that you buy a certain amount of baby equipment specifically for travelling. Apart from the essential pushchair or pram (see Chapter 6), you will need to buy a car seat if you have a car or if you will be getting lifts in a car without a suitable child seat. You may also decide that a baby carrier, or sling, would be a useful means of getting around with your baby, especially during the early weeks. If you want to use a bicycle with your baby, you will need a child seat or a trailer.

There is a wealth of baby travel accessories, designed to make your life easier while you are away from home – these include portable changing mats, in-car bottle-warmers and toys that attach to your baby's car seat. Larger items, such as travel cots and travel highchairs, may prove useful to you if you are going on holiday or staying somewhere overnight.

Car seats

A car seat is one of the very few items you really must buy for your baby if you will be travelling by car. It is illegal to carry a baby in your arms in the front of the car, and not advisable, from a safety point of view, to do this in the back either. If your baby is going to be travelling in a car from day one – for example, from hospital to your home after the birth – you really need to buy a seat *before* the birth. Other equipment can wait, but not a car seat. It is also the only piece of equipment you really should buy new, unless you know with absolute certainty it has never been involved in any sort of crash. A car seat that has been in a crash may have sustained damage that you can't see but which may affect the ability of the seat to protect your child adequately.

Car seats vary considerably in price, and although all seats have to conform to strict safety standards, *Which?* tests (see pages 140–2), have shown that paying more can also mean paying for a safer seat. You'll also be paying more for added extras such as deeper padding, footrests, belt hooks to keep the belt out of the way while you are putting your child in, and additional comfort adjustments.

Seat classifications

Child car seats are split into five different weight categories: 0, 0+, 1, 2 and 3. Check the weight of your child and use the table below to work out which category is most suitable for him or her. Some seats span two or more groups (for example, 0/1 and 0+/1).

Car seat sizes

Weight range	Approximate age range	Group stage/ type of seat
from birth to 10kg	newborn to 9 months	0 rearward-facing
from birth to 13kg	newborn to 15–18 months	0+ rearward-facing
9 kg to 18 kg	9 months to 3–4 years	1 forward-facing
15kg to 25kg	up to 6 years	2 booster seat
22kg to 36kg	up to 11 years	3 booster seat

It can be helpful to put the categories to the back of your mind when buying a seat and to concentrate instead on familiarising yourself with the types of seats available and their characteristics, checking that the ones you like are suitable for your child's weight.

Seat types and sizes

You will probably need to buy two or three types of car seats, as your child grows. There are three basic types of car seat available: infant seats, combination seats and forward-facing seats. (Booster seats, which simply raise the child up so the adult belt can be safely used, are used for older children.) Some seats are designed to stay in the car, while others are lighter and more portable. Some are compatible with pushchairs so you can use them in the car and as a pushchair seat. Decide before you buy which would be best suited to you. As a starting point, for a new baby you need to buy either an infant seat or a combination seat.

Infant seats

These are designed for babies up to 13kg (up to about 15–18 months), depending on the model of seat. They are rearward-facing and have a carrying handle so you can transport your baby to and from the car easily. You use the adult seat belt to hold the seat in position, and your baby is secured to the seat using an integral safety harness. You'll find a wide range of seats for between £40 and £120.

Pros:

✔ you can use the seat to carry your baby to and from the car

✔ it can be a useful additional baby chair for the home

✔ some can be adjusted to have a rocking motion when placed on the floor – helpful for soothing your baby (they provide more support than a bouncy cradle and are suitable for short naps)

✔ some can be fitted on to a pushchair if they are part of a travel system (see pages 176 and 177).

Cons:

✘ if you buy an infant seat, you'll need to buy another seat when your baby gets bigger

✘ new babies can look scrunched-up and uncomfortable because these seats are rarely designed to recline (for safety reasons, the seat shouldn't be shifted to lie in a flatter position while in the car unless it has been specifically designed to allow this) – a head-support cushion can help and these sometimes come with the seat

✘ don't expect it to double up as an extra baby carrier other than to transport your baby to and from the car – it is a fairly heavy piece of equipment and once your baby is past the newborn stage you'll be aching to put it down.

Combination seats

These can be positioned to be either rearward-facing, for a young baby, or forward-facing, for a child who can sit unaided. They can be used from birth until your child weighs about 18kg (about age three to four). The seat is semi-permanently attached to the interior of the car using the adult seat belt, and an integral harness secures the child into the seat. The seats have adjustable seat-recline positions for sleeping. They cost from £50 to £130.

Pros:

✔ in theory, you shouldn't need to buy another seat until your child is ready to move on to a booster seat (see below)

✔ the reclining positions help to make the car ride more comfortable for a sleepy child.

Cons:

✘ during the baby-months these seats are not as portable or versatile as an infant seat – for example, you can't easily move the seat to carry a sleeping baby to and from the car

✘ older children may find some models restrictive and you could end up forking out for another type of seat earlier than you expected.

Forward-facing seats

These seats are for older babies over 9kg (about nine months) and children up to about 25kg (age four to six), depending on the seat. (**Booster seats** are also available for children of about four to eleven – up to 36kg.) This would be the next seat to buy if you start off with an infant seat. There are two basic types – those that are semi-permanently fixed to the car using the adult belt and which have an integral harness to secure your child to the chair, and removable ones that use the adult diagonal belt to secure the child and the seat in the car 'in one'. Both have their advantages and disadvantages.

'Fixed' forward-facing seats have the same appearance as the combination seat (see above), but without the rearward-facing option. You attach the seat to the car interior using the adult belt, and your child is secured in the seat with an integral harness. On some models this harness can be removed when your child gets older and replaced with the adult diagonal belt. These seats can usually be placed in a variety of reclining positions.

Pros:

✔ reclining options mean they can be more comfortable

✔ models that enable you to remove the harness and use the adult belt for older children are more versatile because older children might find a harness over-restricting

✔ many have a high sitting position – good for relieving boredom in smaller children by enabling them to see out of the car window.

Cons:

✗ these seats are generally designed to stay in the car – so can restrict space if, for example, you don't have your child with you and need to give other people a lift

✗ not designed to be portable

✗ more expensive that the other type of forward-facing seat, at £50–170.

Portable forward-facing seats have a more basic design than the fixed type, and use the diagonal adult seat belt to secure the seat and the child 'in one'. You place your child in the seat, pull the adult seat belt through a seat-belt lock near the child's shoulder, pull it across your child then secure it as normal.

Pros:

✔ lightweight and easily portable so can be moved from car to car or thrown in the boot when not being used

✔ the cheapest type of car seat, at £20–90.

Cons:

✗ they don't recline, so younger children may find them less comfortable

✗ the simple design means that they tend not to be as well padded or 'luxurious' as the more expensive forward-facing type of seat

✗ lack of integral harness means that escaping might be easier for some determined children.

Some models of both types of seat have a removable back so that the seat can be turned into a booster cushion for older children. This is a useful extra if you want maximum use out of the seat.

Safety concerns

Tests by Consumers' Association (*Which?*, April 2003 and June 2004) showed that the design of child safety seats is lagging behind improvements in protection for adults in car crashes. For many years Consumers' Association has criticised the official safety test that manufacturers have to put their seats through before they are allowed on to the European market. It says the current test mimics a fairly unrealistic and undemanding front-impact crash. And surprisingly, there is no requirement for child car seats to pass a side-impact test, despite the fact that side impacts are the second most common type of crash (often occurring at junctions).

Which? tested seats for both front and side impacts replicating more true-to-life conditions of what happens to a car in an extreme crash. The results of the tests highlighted weaknesses in many child car seats that would never show up in the standard tests used to certify a seat as safe for sale.

So where does this leave parents who want to buy a safe car seat for their child? It is important to bear in mind that many crashes happen at a lower speed than that at which the seats were tested by *Which?*, and that any properly fitted seat will offer far better protection than not using one at all. Fitting the right size of seat for your car and for your child is a crucial safety measure – experts say that most child deaths in car crashes are caused by seats that haven't been fitted properly, and could be avoided if people bought the right seat for the car and took time to read the instructions and get to know how the seat works. Read the section below on choosing, fitting and using car seats for advice on this.

Which? *Best Buy car seats*
As well as putting the seats through a crash test, *Which?* also assessed the seats for ease of installation, including the quality of the instructions. Which? found that safety standards had improved between 2003 and 2004, and that the Best Buys in 2003, although they still offered the same good protection, were no longer the best you can buy. The Best Buys in 2004 were as follows.

For children up to 13kg (from birth to around 18 months), the Britax Cosy Tot (80 from Babies 'R' Us★ and Boots★) did well in almost all the tests. It was easy to use, with clear instructions. The Maxi Cosi Cabrio (£80 from Babies 'R' Us or £65 from Kiddicare★) and the Mothercare★ Travel Tot (£40) followed close on its heels.

For children from 9kg to 18kg (about nine months to about four years), the Britax Duo Plus Isofix (£180 from John Lewis★, Babies 'R' Us or Mothercare) was the first recommendation. However, it is designed for use with the Isofix fixing system (see page 144), which is found only on newer cars. If your car doesn't have Isofix fittings, go for the Maxi Cosi Priori XP, (£100 from Halfords★ and £94 from

Kiddicare), or the Priori SPS, (£100 from Babies 'R' Us or £75 from Kiddicare).

For children between 15kg and 36kg (about three or four to eleven years old), the Best Buy was the Maxi Cosi Rodi XP, available from Kiddicare (£75), or contact Dorel★ for local stockists. The Best Buy in 2003, the Britax Kid (£79 from John Lewis or £65 from Kiddicare) was deemed to be still a good choice.

Other factors to consider before buying

- Your child's weight, rather than his or her age, is the determining factor when buying or using a car seat.
- Go for removable, machine-washable covers if you can – the seat will get dirty and machine washing is the best way of keeping the covers clean.
- Make a list of the cars in which you might use the child seat – for example, friends' or grandparents' – as well as your own.
- Think about whether you'll need to use the seat with a lap belt in the centre of the rear seat in any of these cars. Not all seats are designed for this. Generally, it's best to use a standard three-point seat belt (or Isofix system) if you can.
- Check with the sales staff that the seat you want is compatible with the make and model of your car. There is no industry standard, which means there is no child seat that fits all cars – although most models will fit most cars. Similarly, if you're buying online or over the phone, check with the seat manufacturers which seats will suit your car.
- Don't use a second-hand car seat. Even if a seat looks undamaged, if it has already been in a crash it may not protect your child. It may also not be built to current safety standards and you are unlikely to have the fitting instructions.

Fitting correctly and maintaining safety

Some car seats are easier to fit properly in your car than others. You must make sure you fit your seat properly. Even if you've bought the safest car seat on the market, if you haven't fitted it correctly, your baby is at risk.

- Ask for a demonstration. Halfords★, for example, offers a child-seat-fitting service in its stores, with trained members of staff.

Other baby-product outlets provide a similar service – the Lilliput★ chain, for example, will fit your car seat even if it hasn't been bought at one of its stores. Make sure you have a go at fitting the seat yourself too, before you buy.

- Follow the instructions carefully when fitting the seat yourself and keep a copy of the instructions in the car. Don't buy the seat if you find the instructions hard to understand. Providing clear instructions is a basic but critical measure that all manufacturers should be getting right.
- Make sure the child seat fits firmly on to the car seat – there should be very little forward or sideways movement. When you open the buckle of the adult belt, a correctly installed seat should spring forward slightly.
- Be careful not to push the seat too hard into the car – for example, by pushing it down with your knee. This could damage the seat.
- Bear in mind other people who will be using the seat – for example, grandparents. If there's anything awkward about fitting the seat, will they be able to install it correctly?
- If the seat has a harness, make sure it is correctly adjusted every time you use it – only one or two fingers should fit between your child's chest and the harness. Position the harness buckle over the hips, not over the stomach.
- If a diagonal seat belt is used, this should rest on the child's shoulder, not on his or her neck.
- The seat belt buckle should be straight when locked. It should not rest on the car-seat frame as this may cause it to snap open in an accident.
- Never modify the seat – for example, by adding extra padding.
- If you have an accident, buy a new seat – the existing one may have been damaged even if this isn't visible.
- Secure your child properly for every journey, no matter how short.

Hired car seats

If you're planning to hire a car on holiday and can't take a baby car seat with you, you'll need to hire one. This should be simple, but in April 2003 researchers from *Which?* found worrying problems when they hired child car seats from a range of car-hire companies in the

The ISOfix system

An attempt has been made by safety experts and some manufacturers to try to resolve the difficulties parents often have with fitting car seats properly by developing a universal standard way to fix seats that can be used by all manufacturers. The difficulty of installing seats is complicated by the fact that many seats fit only particular cars, and many car manufacturers approve only specific seats. The idea behind the ISOfix system is that car manufacturers build mounts into the seats of their cars. The seat manufacturers can then design their seats so that they simply click into place in the car. Safety experts predict that ISOfix will be safer than normal seats as well as easier to fit. The problem is that although ISOfix seats and mounts do exist, both car and seat manufacturers have been slow to support the system – in fact, Consumers' Association says that some car manufacturers are making a mess of implementing it by putting poorly designed mounts in their cars. ISOfix seats are becoming more widely available, so if you have an ISOfix mount in your car, you may feel an ISOfix seat is a good safety option.

Car seats, your baby and the law

By law, you must not allow your baby to travel in the front of a car unless secured in a suitable car seat and, although it is technically legal for you to carry your baby in your arms in the back of a car without a car seat, it is far safer to use one. The seat should be either an infant seat or a combination seat. It must be rearward-facing until your baby reaches 9kg or so (about nine months old) and can sit unaided. You can then use a forward-facing seat. Children under the age of three travelling in the back of the car are only legally required to use a seat where one is available – although, for safety's sake, any sensible parent would make sure one is available. Children under the age of three travelling in the front seat of a car must be seated in a car seat suitable for their weight; an adult belt on its own is not acceptable.

UK, Greece and Spain. Many of the seats provided were so out of date they didn't meet modern safety standards. Some had bits broken through wear and tear. Where the hire outlets fitted the seats for the researchers, they were often fitted incorrectly. Many outlets, especially those in the UK, expect you to fit the seat yourself but the *Which?* researchers found they often failed to provide adequate instructions to enable parents to fit the seat properly. Children's lives are being put at risk because of these practices by hire companies. *Which?* has taken up the issue with the trade body representing car-hire companies in the UK. If you're not happy with the seat provided by your car-hire company, it is safest to buy a new seat yourself at your destination. Although this is an expensive option, new seats for sale have to pass modern safety tests so you'll be protecting your baby properly. If this isn't an option for you, bear in mind that any seat is better than no seat at all.

Car seats on aeroplanes

The safest way for a child aged between six months and two years to travel on a plane is using a child restraint – either a car seat provided by you or a restraint provided by the airline. This is the theory. The reality is that your car seat will not necessarily be suitable for use on

Safety watch

The safest place for a child's car seat is the centre of the rear seat (this way it is protected from side impact). If it is not possible to put the seat here, an outside rear seat is the next best option. The front passenger seat should be your last choice, although many parents find it more practical to have a young baby next to them rather than behind them.

Infant seats and portable forward-facing seats are suitable for use in the front or back of the car; combination and fixed forward-facing seats can generally be used in the front seat but this depends on the model of car seat.

Never use a child car seat on a front passenger seat fitted with an airbag that hasn't been deactivated. In the event of a crash, the airbag could result in the serious injury or death of the child. Airbags are especially dangerous with rearward-facing car seats but the rule applies to forward-facing seats too.

the plane, and not all airlines provide their own restraints. Sitting on their parent's lap with a loop-extension belt, which is what a lot of young children end up doing, is second best in terms of safety. Children between the ages of two and three must sit in their own seat with a special belt, or in a child restraint. Babies under six months old are too small to sit in a separate seat, so generally must sit on your lap – although some airlines have a limited number of baby 'cradles' fitted in specific sections of the plane. Once your child is three, there are no special requirements.

If you are travelling on a plane with a child under three, talk through the seating options with the airline or travel agent. If you are planning to use a car seat, check that it will be suitable for use on the plane. You will need to book early if you want to use an airline's child restraints (and remember that not all provide them) – if you just turn up there may not be enough available on the plane.

Another option is to buy your own restraint – Urchin★ sells a 'flight vest' (£26.95) so your baby can sit on your lap and also be properly restrained.

Car accessories

There can't be many parents of babies and young children who have avoided the experience of a car journey from hell. Although a gently humming engine has wonderful sleep-inducing powers, especially in the early months, a bored, grouchy or mischievous child strapped into the back can easily turn a run-of-the-mill journey into a stress-filled rollercoaster ride. Toys can become missiles, supposedly secure seat belts get undone, crying can seem non-stop and there is always the threat of a projectile vomit or a particularly unfortunate 'toilet accident' in the middle of a rush-hour traffic jam.

Some of these situations are more or less unavoidable, and parents can only try their utmost to stay cool, calm and collected in the most trying conditions. For others, however, manufacturers have come up with a range of products designed to help alleviate the stress of fretful journeys. Gadgets range from rear-seat mirrors, so you can see what is going on in the back without turning round, to sleep-inducing comfort cushions.

A basic car survival kit

As a starting point, it is worth putting together your own 'car survival kit' that you keep in the car permanently, making sure you renew the contents as and when necessary. All this needs to contain are a few basic items which you feel could be useful to you in some situations. Obviously the contents will vary depending on the child's needs and age, but a selection along the following lines could prove handy:

- spare nappies
- a packet of wipes
- nappy sacks
- a muslin cloth or small towel (especially useful as a quickly grabbable cleaning aid after a bout of sickness)
- tempting snacks (but nothing your child could choke on)
- spare dummies
- a couple of picture books and toys
- a change of clothes (and maybe a spare top for you too).

Some items can be packed away in the boot or in a bag, but some, such as the snacks or the dummies, you will want to keep within arm's reach.

Accessories to consider

Think about your own and your child's needs and foibles before you fork out on a range of car accessories – in order to avoid having a car stuffed with supposedly innovative and 'essential' items that are simply ignored or abused.

Seat-belt safety

Your innocent baby could easily turn into a seat-belt escapee once he or she has the curiosity and dexterity to work out the seat-belt mechanism. A number of products are designed to make undoing the seat-belt buckle more difficult. The Safeclip, for example, (£5.99 from The Great Little Trading Company*), is a plastic see-through clip that slides over the seat-belt buckle – when you want to undo the buckle, you slide the clip out of the way). A similar product is the Seat Belt Buckle Protector (£4.99 from JoJo Maman Bébé*).

Other seat-belt products are designed to improve the fit of the belt. For example, the Mighty-Tite Seat Securer (£14.99 from JoJo Maman Bébé) is a ratchet mechanism device that allows you easily to tighten slack on seat belts securing a car seat.

Sunblinds

Car sunblinds can be very useful for helping children sleep on bright days and simply for stopping the sun from shining in their eyes. You usually attach the sunblinds to the side back window, using either suction pads or clips. Some models are designed like household blinds and can be rolled up when you don't need to use them. Others are simply taken on and off the window as and when needed. Those that use suction pads need to be placed on a clean window otherwise the pads may not stick. All can provide a certain level of amusement if within reach of curious fingers, so may not be as durable or stay up for as long as you might hope. You can also buy sun canopies that fit over infant car seats. Try Mothercare★ or car accessory shops such as Halfords★ for a selection of these products. You can also buy a sun shade designed specifically to fit over the car seat – by Cheeky Rascals★.

Sleep cushions

Cushioned neck rolls can prevent your child's head from lolling from side to side when he or she is in a deep slumber. Some of these come in the form of cuddly toys so may provide a degree of entertainment. The main drawback is that some children don't like wearing them. Neck cushions are widely available from children's stores.

You can also buy support cushions for older children who use a booster seat. The cheaper version is a cushion 'roll' which fits over the seat belt in a position that enables your child to rest his or her head against the cushion (they are widely available – expect to pay about £5). A more expensive option is a design with two head cushions positioned on either side of a piece of padded fabric, which fits behind your child's head and back (Mothercare★ sells one for £10).

Rear-view mirrors

Turning around when you are driving, because your baby has made an unfamiliar sound or your toddler is complaining, is a dangerous response that a rear-view mirror can help you avoid. Depending on the model, you can fit this over your existing mirror or position it with suction pads in an appropriate place on the windscreen. Some give you a panoramic view of the traffic behind and are usually made up of one wide mirror for the traffic with a smaller one directed at the back seat. Others are designed to give you a view of just the back seat. Don't expect a perfect view of your child, however – it depends where in the back your child is sitting, and front-seat headrests can partially obscure the view. Try Boots★, Mothercare★ and car accessory shops or contact The Great Little Trading Company★ for a panoramic view model at £7.99, or JoJo Maman Bébé★ for a suction model at £3.99.

Staying snug

You can, of course, just use a good old spare blanket – but, needless to say, a range of products are available for keeping your baby cosy on cold car journeys. You can buy a wide range of fleeces and blankets that fit into or over a car seat. You can also buy covers to protect your baby from the wind or rain while being carried along in the car seat. These are normally designed to fit baby car seats with rigid handles. They are widely available from children's stores – Mothercare★ sells a car accessory set which has a wind and rain cover, a 'cosy toes' and a head support cushion for £20.

Keeping clean

Sticky fingers and grubby shoes will soon turn the car into a pit. You could put up with it and have a clean-up whenever you get the chance, or you could be extra-vigilant and try to ensure that faces and fingers are wiped, shoes are removed and food and drink are banned before putting your children in the car. Alternatively, you could buy some car interior 'protectors'. These are wipe-clean bits of plastic of various shapes and forms designed to shield your seats. Blooming Marvellous★ and JoJo Maman Bébé★ sell a back-seat protector for £5.99 which fits over the front-seat headrest and prevents your child's kicking feet from soiling the back of the seat (it doesn't stop the kicking, though!). You can also buy large wipe-clean mats that fit under and around your child's seat, ensuring that he or she is surrounded by a cleanable zone. To protect your seats from toilet accidents and drinks spills, you can buy absorbent but stay-dry cushions that fit into a car seat (Boots★ sells one for £7 – try its website if your local store doesn't have them).

Food and drink

You can buy car bottle-warmers, which plug into the car cigarette lighter – for details of these see page 109. For older children, there are special food and drink holders that you attach to the door or to the back of the front seat so (theoretically at least) children can rest their drinks without spilling them and save half-eaten snacks for later rather than letting them drop on the floor. Try the Car Snack Tray from JoJo Maman Bébé★, at £4.99.

Storage solutions

There are various storage products to help keep under control the mass of toys, books and other bits and pieces that can easily build up in your car when you have children. A car tidy or organiser, for example, fits over a front seat headrest and has a range of different-sized pockets for all your essentials. These are useful for older children or if you are sitting in the back with your child and want to have everything within reach. They are not particularly handy, however, when you are in the front. Try car accessory shops; alternatively, Babies 'R' Us★ sells one for £9.99.

One storage item you won't need to spend money on is a simple bag for rubbish – having a bag to throw everything into, particularly on long car journeys, can give you at least some sense of order. You *can* buy special car litter containers that fit over the front-seat headrest (£9.99 from The Great Little Trading Company★), but a plastic bag will do the job perfectly well.

In-car toys and entertainment

If your child has a favourite toy, it's worth making sure you have it at hand on car journeys. Some toys, however, are designed specifically for travel use. Because babies tend to drop their toys and cry to get them back, many of these car toys can be attached to your child's seat or the car interior, or to your child. The following are some examples.

- Mothercare★ Cat and Dog Car Bar (£14.99) – this mini baby gym has colourful animal characters attached to a padded bar, which you place over the car seat within easy reach for patting and tweaking. Other manufacturers produce similar products.
- Velcro-fastening rattles – these are handy for the car because the rattle, usually in the form of a soft animal, is attached to a Velcro band which you put around your baby's wrist. Your baby can't drop the rattle and should have fun waving his or her arms around to make the rattle 'rattle'. Widely available from nursery stores.
- Car Seat Gallery – a range of cards showing simple patterns and pictures (either black and white or in bold colours) that you slot into a transparent plastic folder and attach to the back or front of a front seat, depending on where your child is sitting. The idea is that babies will enjoy studying the contrasting lights and darks of the patterns and will recognise the simple shapes. The graphics are based on results of research into what young babies can see. You can also place photographs of family members, for example, in the slots. Priced at around £15, they are widely available from children's stores, or try Blooming Marvellous★, JoJo Maman Bébé★ or Krucial Kids★.
- Shake, rattle and roll toys – a selection of colourful soft animal-shaped toys that you 'hook' on to a car seat canopy. You can buy them from Blooming Marvellous★ for £16.99 each.
- Suction toys – you can buy a range of toys that stick to the car window within reach of your baby. Try the 'Drivetime Mouse' at £15.99 from **www.travellingwithchildren.co.uk**.

If toys don't seem to do the trick, music tapes or CDs or – for older children – simple story tapes can be good entertainment value. These are widely available in children's music and book shops.

Baby carriers

When your baby is small, a baby carrier, or sling, is a useful way of going out and about with minimal hassle. With both hands free and without having to manage a pram or pushchair, you'll have more freedom to do the shopping, negotiate public transport, load up the car, etc. If you have a toddler as well as a baby, you can go out with the baby carrier and the buggy, avoiding – or at least postponing – the need to buy a double pushchair. Even when you are in the house, a carrier can prove handy. Babies are often soothed by being so close to a warm body, so you can use the carrier to calm your baby while you are doing the housework or gardening.

Bear in mind that some babies simply don't like baby carriers. This is less the case when they are very young, but once they start becoming mobile the protests at being 'harnessed' into a carrier can start. Consider this if you are thinking of buying a model designed to cope with a wide age range (some can carry a compliant child well into the toddler years). Unfortunately there's no way of knowing how your older baby will take to a carrier – it's a case of buy before you try. Remember, too, that however well designed a carrier is, depending on your own stature and the weight of your baby, using one may simply become more and more uncomfortable for you as your baby grows. Having said that, many parents continue to find carriers a useful additional mode of transport for older babies and toddlers.

Types of baby carrier
There are three main carrier types available, the major difference between these being the various positions in which they enable you to carry your baby.

Two-way carriers
These are the simplest and most widely available carriers. A two-way carrier harnesses your baby in front of you, either with his or her face inwards towards your chest or facing outwards to view the world. A padded headrest supports the head; this can normally be folded down for an older baby. You adjust the carrier depending on what suits your baby – the facing-inward position is for newborns but once your baby can support his or her head, the facing-outward position is better. These carriers are generally suitable for babies up to about nine months.

Pros:
✔ two positions are sufficient for most parents and younger babies
✔ tend to be cheaper than the alternatives, at around £20.

Cons:
✘ not as versatile as other carriers.

Multi-way carriers

With this type, depending on the model, in addition to being able to carry your baby upright on your front, you can carry him or her in a nursing, or 'cradle' position; on your back; or at your side, 'hipster' style. Many models offer just three positions – usually to carry your baby on your front, back or in a nursing position. Four-way carriers let your baby go on your front or back, or in the nursing or hip position.

Most multi-way carriers are of a similar design to the two-way carrier and have a 'harness'-style appearance. Others are more like traditional slings and are hammock-style: a large piece of thick fabric holds your baby and continues around your shoulders – you adjust the sling by pulling the fabric through a pair of strong plastic rings. Multi-way carriers tend to be designed for babies from birth to either 12 months, 18 months or to a 14kg toddler, depending on the model.

Harness-style carriers are widely available from children's stores. The sling-style may be more difficult to come by and some are available by mail order only. Examples of the sling style include the Huggababy★ or The Better Baby Sling★. Another type of multi-way carrier, which is a cross between a harness and a sling, is the Wilkinet★ brand – this has a harness but no leg holes and the baby is supported by long straps that wrap around you both (available by mail order from Wilkinet).

Pros:
✔ more versatile than two-way carriers
✔ longer lifespan
✔ those offering a nursing position can be particularly handy for breast-feeding.

Cons:
✘ tend to be more expensive than two-way carriers, at £30–50
✘ some, particularly the sling style, can take a bit of practice to use correctly (a few brands come with instructional videos)
✘ lifespan may be limited by the recalcitrance of an older baby or toddler.

Back-only carriers

These carriers are generally aimed at babies from six months, because they need to be able to support themselves sitting up –

although a handful are designed for younger babies. The carriers have a rucksack-style appearance: your baby sits in a harness, supported either by a lightweight metal frame or rigid rucksack-style padding, and the carrier is put on using padded shoulder straps and a waist belt. Your baby will be positioned with his or her head and shoulders just above your shoulders. Those models at the top end of the market are made by outdoor clothing and equipment specialists. Some have a fair amount of storage space, for clothing and food, for example, and with some models you can buy extras such as sun and rain covers. As long as your child is willing, you can use most models until the age of two-and-a-half or three.

Pros:

✔ the above-the-shoulder position is popular with babies and toddlers because they are high enough to get a grown-up view of the world (the back position of the fabric multi-way carriers, in contrast, tends to be lower down, so your baby's view is restricted)

✔ parents who want regularly to take their child on walks or hikes can get carriers designed specifically with their needs in mind – for example, extra-lightweight and comfortable carriers with weatherproof features

✔ carriers with a metal frame are usually designed so you can stand the carrier upright on its own – making it easier to get your child in and out and useful for standing the carrier up on its own when you need a rest (although you must not leave your child unattended in a carrier).

Cons:

✘ be prepared for pain! – some babies will never tire of pulling your hair and ears from their superb hard-for-you-to-reach vantage position at the back (using a sun/rain cover is one way of ensuring this doesn't happen)

✘ you may well need another person around to help you put the carrier on and take it off, so it might not be ideal for use on your own – unless you find it manageable to put on and take off by resting it on a seat

✗ tend to be the most expensive type of carrier available – although you can get basic models that are fine for strolls (for example, Mothercare★ sells a framed back carrier for £30), you can easily pay over £150 for a top-of-the-range model aimed at serious walkers.

> 66 With my first baby I used a multi-way sling carrier almost constantly for the first months. He wanted to breast-feed a lot so it was really easy for me to feed him while he was still in the sling, and he could do this more or less wherever we were. With my second baby it has been less useful, simply because he doesn't feed as much. 99
>
> Gillian, mother of Seku, 6 months and Ian, 4

Other points to consider before you buy

- You need to feel secure and comfortable with your baby in the carrier. If you can, try out a selection of carriers with your baby in them to see which feels most comfortable for you.
- Even if you can't try carriers out with your baby inside, try a selection on anyway to see how you get on with fastening devices and position adjustments. If anything seems over-fiddly to you or if you think you'll have trouble putting a carrier on properly, move on to another one (although bear in mind that some types simply need a bit of practice to get right).
- Look for shoulder straps that are wide and well-padded.
- Your baby needs comfort too – if there are leg holes, check these are well-padded and that there is good support and padding for your baby's back and – for younger babies in particular – head.
- Think about whether you need a carrier with added 'bits and bobs', such as a 'soother pouch' or a 'dribble bib' – some models have these and you may find them useful.
- Check whether the carrier is machine-washable (the back-only sort is not). It is bound to get dribbled or vomited on at some point, so anything that is sponge-clean only won't stay as fresh as one that you can simply throw in the washing machine.

Travel highchairs

Travel or portable highchairs are useful if you are likely to be visiting child-free relatives or friends on a regular basis, travelling to holiday homes or visiting cafés and restaurants that don't make provision for babies. There are various types available, ranging from table-top fabric chairs that screw to the table to fold-up booster seats and harness-style models that secure your child to an ordinary dining chair. They are mostly lightweight and fold up easily – some types can even fit into a handbag. As with ordinary highchairs (see pages 120–8), travel highchairs are only suitable for babies who can sit unaided.

Some parents use a travel highchair instead of a standard highchair in their own home. If you are short on space or money (they are a lot cheaper than most normal highchairs), or simply want to avoid any extra clutter, most travel highchairs are perfectly acceptable to use at home. You just need to make sure the model you want fits your particular type of table or chairs.

If you are planning to buy a travel highchair specifically for use on a holiday, bear in mind that lots of holiday homes and hotels will provide a highchair anyway, so check this out before you buy.

Types of travel highchair

Table seats
The usual design of this type is a seat of washable fabric secured around a metal frame. You screw or clip the seat to the table-top and your child sits in the seat and eats at the table with his or her legs dangling underneath. Your child should be secured with a safety harness. When you first use one you may feel it is unsafe because your child's legs are not taking any of the weight, but the chairs are designed such that, as long as the table is stable, your child's weight is balanced and supported. Once you have finished with it, you unscrew the seat and fold it flat. This sort of seat costs around £25.

Pros:
✔ easy to fit
✔ takes up minimal space as you don't need a dining chair as well
✔ fits most types of table.

Cons:

✗ the metal frame means this type isn't really light enough if you want to carry it around in a bag

✗ dangerous if fitted to an unsuitable table as baby and table could flip over – you must only use this type of seat on a solid table that has the top attached to the base, and not on glass tables, lightweight tables (picnic tables, for example), single pedestal tables or tables with a bevelled edge. These restrictions will be made clear in the seat's instructions.

Folding booster seats

This is a sturdy plastic seat that you place on a conventional dining chair and attach with straps to the back and bottom of the chair. Some also have rubber pads on the seat base for extra security. The booster seat raises your child to a comfortable table level. Some models have removable trays and most have adjustable seat heights.

Pros:

✔ lets your child feel that he or she is sitting in a 'grown-up' chair

✔ adjustable seat heights and removable tray means you have a number of seating options

✔ tend to be slightly cheaper than table seats (Mothercare★ sells one for £21.99, as opposed to £24.99 for a table seat)

✔ wipe-clean plastic, so easy to keep clean (some can be folded up to put in a dishwasher).

Cons:

✗ not as compact as a table seat and too bulky and heavy to be carried around

✗ you need to be careful to fit it only on to a sturdy, stable dining chair; it's not for use on stools or low-backed chairs.

Fold-flat travel highchairs

This is a conventional-looking plastic highchair designed to be extra-lightweight and fold extra-flat so that it is easily packed away.

Pros:

✔ a good choice if you or your baby feels more at home with a conventional highchair

✔ fairly cheap – around the same price as table seats and booster seats (e.g. £24.99 from Babies 'R' Us★)

✔ useful if you don't want to risk a travel or booster seat being unsuitable for the furnishings in the place you are staying.

Cons:

✘ length-wise it still takes up the space of a normal highchair, so not as portable as the alternatives.

'Harness' seats

In this type of chair, a fabric harness fits on to a normal dining chair and you seat your child in the harness. Designs vary – some have a 'hood'-style back that you slide over the top of the chair, others have a harness attached to a wide strap that you Velcro around the back of the chair, and another is a padded back-and-seat cushion with a standard harness.

Pros:

✔ truly portable, these seats are lightweight enough to fold away into a bag and carry around

✔ usually machine-washable.

Cons:

✘ designed for occasional rather than daily use

✘ your child will not be raised to table height so will not be able to use the table surface to eat (using a couple of cushions might be one way round this)

✘ less widely available than previous types – try JoJo Maman Bébé★ or Blooming Marvellous★, or contact Clippasafe★ for details of its Dining Chair Harness.

'Hook on' travel seats

This is an innovative style of seat from a company in Denmark. The HandySitt is a wooden geometrically shaped seat that you hook over the back of a dining chair; the short legs are adjusted so they sit on the dining chair seat. You sit your child in the seat and secure him or her with a harness (a removable one is supplied). The seat folds flat for travelling and you can buy a separate travel bag.

Pros:

✔ unusual, modern design that may be attractive to style-conscious parents

✔ good lifespan – it fits children aged from six months to four years.

Cons:

✘ expensive compared with other seats (around £50) so probably uneconomical for occasional travel use

✘ won't fit some types of chair.

Travel cots

Travel cots are portable cots that you can fold up and put in a bag to take away with you. Most have a plastic or metal frame, woven fabric-and-mesh sides, and a hard segmented bottom with a folding, lightly padded mattress. They generally fold and unfold using a central locking system: you pull up a ring or handle in the centre of the base, click the sides into place, then push the handle back down to keep the locked sides rigid. A few models fold flat – these don't come with a bag and may not fold compactly enough to fit into the boot of the car, so are less suitable for travel (although they are fine as an extra cot for guest babies).

Some travel cot models can double up as playpens, although they won't provide as much space as conventional models (for more on playpens, see pages 205–7). Some come with a bassinette for newborns, but generally they are not designed for very young babies as they do not have drop-down sides or adjustable mattress heights. A soft carry cot or Moses basket (See pages 68–9) can be just as portable but more suitable for newborns, and you can also buy lightweight fold-up travel carry cots from a range of baby catalogues.

Many parents get a lot of use out of travel cots. They can give you the freedom of staying almost wherever you want without having to worry about where the baby will sleep. A travel cot can also provide an extra sleeping place for babies who come to stay at your home. The playpen-sized models have even more potential for regular use.

Equally, however, countless travel cots are only ever used a handful of times. They can take up a fair amount of storage space even when folded into the bag, and even though they are portable they can be heavy to carry around. They cost on average between £40 and £80 – so you really don't want to buy one unless you are sure you'll get some decent use out of it. In other words, you only really need one if you will be making regular overnight trips to cot-free homes. Even then, if your baby is likely to stay somewhere overnight on a regular basis (say, at grandparents'), it is worth considering buying a cheap standard cot instead to keep at their house – Ikea* sells a basic cot for around £30). If you plan to stay at a hotel or holiday home, many will provide a cot anyway or at least will be able to arrange hiring one for you. And if you have a network of friends with young children, borrowing a travel cot for occasional use shouldn't be too hard.

If you decide a travel cot would be useful for you, bear the following points in mind when choosing one.

- Some cots have wheels. This is a useful extra feature if you are likely to need to move the cot around. Wheels on the bag – either separate from those on the cot or poking from the cot through the bag – can be especially useful, as travel cots are often heavy to carry.
- Weight and size are important. Some travel cots are more spacious than others. Look at the measurements – you may want to choose a larger size if you plan to use the cot as a playpen. Cot weights can vary a lot too. You'll probably appreciate a lighter one if you plan to travel by public transport or plane, rather than by car; however, these are also likely to be smaller. The weight should be labelled on the cot's instructions or specifications.
- Folding mechanisms can be fiddly, although practice is often all that is needed. Try unfolding, folding and lifting a few cots in the shop before you buy. If this isn't possible, ask whether you can return the cot if you're not happy with the folding mechanism once you have practised at home.
- If you want the cot to double as a playpen, then four rather than two mesh sides will give you and your baby a better view. Some models have a blind that can be rolled down one of the sides so that distractions are kept to a minimum when you want your baby to rest.

- Some models have a range of extra features, such as a changing mat that fits over the top of the cot, sun-blinds and toy storage pockets. Think about whether you will use these – you may be paying extra unnecessarily.
- Look for a removable frame cover and mattress cover, for easy washing.
- Clear, permanent instructions printed on the base of the cot are more useful than an instruction leaflet that you can easily lose.

Second-hand travel cots

Because travel cots may be used only occasionally it is tempting to buy second-hand. This is fine – but bear the following advice in mind.

- Ask for the original instructions if there is nothing printed on the cot.
- Check for obvious damage, such as holes in the mesh sides.
- Check that the mattress is in good condition. It may be hard to get a new one the right size and it is very important that you don't use a mattress that isn't a proper fit (see 'Mattresses', pages 73–8). Furthermore, travel cots don't all have the same basic dimensions and the way the mattress folds is integral to the packing-away process – so one that is the wrong size can make it difficult to store neatly.
- Check the base for damage and the frame for flaking paint and sharp edges.
- If the cot looks fine, try folding and unfolding it several times to check that it locks securely into place every time.

Cycling with your baby

If you used a bike a lot for transport before you had your baby, there's no reason to stop using it after he or she is born. As long as you have the right equipment, cycling with your baby can be a quick and convenient way of getting out and about. You may have to wait a while, however. For obvious safety reasons, it's not recommended that you take a baby who cannot support his or her own head out with you on a bike – as until this time he or she won't be able to wear a cycling helmet. Ideally, your baby should also be able to sit well and unaided. Baby bike seats tend to be designed for use by babies from about six months of age. Trailers, designed to carry one or two children, are also available. Whichever option you are interested in, check with the bike retailer that your bike is suitable for use with a child seat or trailer, as not all bike designs are appropriate.

Once your baby is old enough to go with you on your bike, you have a choice from the following seat options.

Rear-mounted seats

These are the most widely used bike seats. They fit over the back wheel and will usually have a high back and raised sides.

Pros:
- ✔ high back and sides mean that younger children are well supported if they want to sleep while you are cycling
- ✔ you can use the seat to carry shopping when you don't have your child with you.

Cons:
- ✘ carrying extra weight on the back of the bike, especially if your child is moving around, can make stability a problem
- ✘ you can't see what your child is up to or talk to him or her very easily while you are cycling.

Front-mounted seats

With this type of seat your child sits in front of you and you place your arms around the seat to hold the handlebars. Because your arms have to go around the seat and your vision of the road needs to be clear, front-mounted seats are more compact than rear-mounted seats.

Pros:
- ✔ you have closer contact with your child, so can chat with and have better control of him or her as you are cycling
- ✔ stability can be easier to maintain because the extra weight is at the front.

Cons:

✗ although popular in mainland Europe, these seats are less generally available in the UK than rear-mounted seats and may be hard to find (the Centric Safe Haven is an award-winning Canadian brand that has recently become available – try bike specialists **www.realcycles.com** or **www.kidsonthe move.co.uk**).

Bicycle trailers

With these, you tow your child behind you in an enclosed 'carriage'. This has two bicycle-type wheels and a long hitching arm that fastens to your bike. Your child is seated and strapped in inside the zippered, weatherproof and ventilated compartment, which has fabric or plastic windows so that he or she can see out as you are cycling.

Pros:

✔ your child should have a decent amount of space inside the trailer, with reasonable leg room, comfy seating and storage places for toys

✔ two-seaters are widely available, so you can cycle with two small children

✔ you will probably feel more stable cycling with a trailer than with a bike seat because the extra weight isn't directly on the bike

✔ with some makes (Burley trailers, for example), you can buy a special handle attachment to convert the trailer into a pushchair.

Cons:

✗ you won't have the same physical closeness to your child as you would with a bike seat

✗ although any trailer used on the road should have a tall pennant and rear lighting so that it is clearly visible to motorists, the fact that your child is seated at quite a low level can make him or her appear vulnerable, and you may feel happier using the trailer 'off road' – for example, in a park – rather than as a practical travel solution to get from A to B

✗ trailers can tip over, especially when turning abruptly or going over bumps

✗ they can be expensive – expect to pay about £300–400 – and you will need to consider whether you will use the trailer enough to justify the price.

Changing bags

New parents often regard a changing bag as a 'must have' item. These bags do have advantages – for example, wipe-clean compartments that are just the right size for nappies, bottles and other baby essentials, and a portable changing mat. When you are getting to grips with all the extra organisation involved in taking a baby out for an afternoon, a handy bag designed specifically for baby paraphernalia is one thing that can help the day run smoothly (as long as you keep it stocked up, that is). Having said that, it's not as if an ordinary, relatively roomy bag can't do the job of carrying your baby's things. Any bag that can hold a few nappies and wipes, a bottle or two, a change of baby clothes and a travel changing mat, plus a few of your own bits and pieces, will do just fine. How necessary a changing bag is depends on whether you are a minimalist parent who likes to stick to the bare essentials or whether you like the idea of the full baby kit.

Changing bags are widely available. Style-wise, you can choose from shoulder bags or rucksacks, with designs from frills and motifs to smart, matt-black models.

Things to bear in mind when buying

- Choose a bag that is washable as it is bound to get grubby.
- Check that the straps seem secure and the bag appears durable – you'll be hauling it around on a daily basis so you don't want the straps hanging off by the third month.
- You don't need countless internal compartments and pockets – this makes it easier to lose track of what you've put where, which can be highly irritating when, for example, you need some wipes in a hurry. In many ways, the more simple the bag, the better.
- Some bags have large bottle-insulating compartments – these are potentially useful for bottle-fed babies but are not necessary if you are breast-feeding.
- Rucksack-style bags have an advantage in that they are less likely to get in your way – however, they are not as easy to hang on the pram or pushchair.

- If both you and your partner will be using the bag when out and about, you may want to choose a unisex design – there are lots of sporty styles out there.
- If you like to keep your own things separate but in the same bag, some bags have special pockets for your own items, such as a mobile phone or loose change.

Holidays with a baby

When you first go on holiday with your baby, you'll be amazed at all the extra baggage you find yourself taking with you. From travel cots to portable highchairs to favourite toys or blankets . . . the list of items can go on and on unless you sit down and think about what you really need and what you can do without for a couple of weeks. Consider the following travelling tips.

- Check what baby equipment the company you are travelling with, or the place you are travelling to, can provide. If you are hiring a cottage, for example, items such as highchairs and cots are often provided and, if not, you can normally hire such equipment through the holiday home company. If you are travelling abroad with a tour operator you will probably be able to hire cots and even buggies through them, as many pride themselves on the baby-friendliness of their resorts. Alternatively, you can contact the local tourist office.
- You don't need everything you use at home and you can make substitutions – for example, you could use the child car seat as a feeding chair, or a baby carrier instead of a pushchair for getting out and about; and use boiling water in a pan instead of a space-consuming steriliser for sterilising bottles (see pages 103–7).
- Borrow rather than buy if you don't want to increase your holiday budget. If you know someone with a travel cot or a spare, lightweight buggy, for example, there's no harm in asking.
- If you do decide to buy new, bear in mind that you'll probably only be using the item(s) occasionally after your holiday, so basic rather than top-of-the-range is likely to be adequate. A possible exception to this is if you are buying your first umbrella-folding stroller (see pages 180–2) to go on holiday.

There's a fair chance that you will be using this regularly at some point, once you or your baby 'grow out of' your current mode of pushchair transport. The most basic strollers, although fine as a spare, can be quite heavy and tend to be less user-friendly than the slightly more sophisticated models. Paying a little bit more for a lighter-weight model with a few extra features is worth considering.

- If you are bottle-feeding, buying cartons of ready-mixed baby milk (ideally at your destination since they are heavy) will save you time and hassle if you need milk while you are on the beach or out and about.

- Disposable items of baby equipment, although not particularly environmentally friendly, can make your life easier on holiday – see page 101 for details of disposable bottles and disposable bibs and, if you normally use washable nappies, pages 30–2, 37 and 38 for details of disposable nappies, including 'greener' disposables.

- Travel versions of various types of baby equipment are widely available (although think hard whether you really need to buy) – see earlier in this chapter for details of travel highchairs and travel cots/playpens, page 106 for travel sterilisers and travel bottle-warmers, and page 210 for travel potties.

- The most popular nappy brands are available in most foreign resorts, so if you need to restrict your luggage it's worth buying them once you get there. However, they can be more expensive than in the UK. If you're travelling abroad by car, in particular, consider taking a full supply of nappies with you.

Staying safe in the sun

It is vital that you protect your baby's skin from the sun. Small babies need to be kept out of the sun completely. It is harder to do this with toddlers and babies on the move, so you need to be vigilant. Use the following.

- **Sun hat** – this is essential for sun protection. With older babies or toddlers you'll probably have to wrestle with them to keep it on their head, so a hat with ties or an elasticated fit can help to resist determined little hands. 'Legionnaire' styles with a flap at the back are widely available and are very effective at protecting the whole head and neck. Wide-brimmed hats are a good alternative. Other styles – for example, a straightforward baseball cap design – won't provide the necessary protection.

- **Sun-safe clothing** – a T-shirt often isn't enough to protect a child's skin from burning as it can still let through harmful ultraviolet (UV) rays. If you want to be sure of maximum protection, you can buy special clothes which guarantee to let through only the tiniest amounts of UV rays. Look for clothes with the label 'prevents sunburn'. Clothes with this claim will have reached British Standard 7949, which sets a strict sun protection standard for children's clothes.

- **Sun cream** – choose a cream with a sun protection factor (SPF) of between 15 and 30. The SPF should be clearly displayed on the label. Many sun creams aimed at children will have an SPF higher than 30, but they won't actually give your child much more protection in real terms. A 20-point increase in the SPF number doesn't give a corresponding increase in protection. There is concern that buying sun creams with a higher SPF than 30 lulls parents into a false sense of security about how long their children can be exposed to the sun – in Australia, for example, 30+ is the highest SPF allowed – and Consumers' Association believes that SPF labels above 30 should be banned in the UK too. It's also worth avoiding very cheap, little-known creams: tests by trading standards officers and Consumers' Association (*Which?*, June 2001) have found some of these to have far lower levels of sun protection than is claimed on the label. Stick to well-known brands or, for good value for money for the same level of protection, own-label chain-store products such as those made by Boots★, Superdrug or supermarkets.

- **First-aid kit** – see pages 198 and 199 for details.

Other beach accessories

- **Swim nappies** – these are useful if you don't want your child in normal nappies on the beach and don't want to risk any 'accidents' in the water. They have a sewn-in nylon mesh to keep poo inside. Travel companies and hotels will often insist that non-toilet-trained children wear swim nappies in swimming pools, and ordinary trunks and swimming costumes will not be acceptable. Swim nappies are widely available – the Kooshies brand is a popular make and an originator of the swim nappy concept. Swim nappies with ties or side-snap fastenings will be easier to change than pull-on-and-off styles. It's best to buy two swim nappies so one can dry while the other is in use. You can also buy packs of disposable swim nappies (available from most supermarkets), although these can work out expensive and a fairly bulky item to take away with you if you need to minimise your luggage.

- **Baby wetsuits** – these allow your baby to stay playing in the water for longer. They open at the bottom for easy changing. JoJo Maman Bébé★ sells one for babies of 6–24 months for £24.99.

- **Buoyancy aids** – older children can have armbands but babies needn't miss out on the joys of floating in the water. You can buy baby swim floats, which have an integral shaped baby seat with leg holes. Your baby sits in the seat with his or her back and chest supported and can splash about and kick safely (with, of course, an adult supervising). Buoyancy aids come in different sizes and are suitable for babies from about three months. They are widely available.

- **Sun-safe tents/cabanas** – these pop-up, pod-shaped, open-sided tents are ideal for keeping a young baby properly in the shade when on the beach, and offer high levels of UV protection. You can buy family-sized as well as child-sized tents so adults can sit in the shade too. They are widely available from nursery and department stores.

If you want more information on hotels and travel companies which cater for babies and ideas for baby-friendly holidays, plus more information on products that may be of help on your travels, look up the specialist travel websites **www.babygoes2.com** or **www.travellingwithchildren.co.uk.**

Websites

Babies 'R' Us	www.babiesrus.co.uk
Babygoes2	www.babygoes2.com
The Better Baby Sling	www.betterbabysling.co.uk
Blooming Marvellous	www.bloomingmarvellous.co.uk
Boots	www.boots.com
Cheeky Rascals	www.cheekyrascals.co.uk
Clippasafe	www.clippasafe.co.uk
Dorel	www.dorel.com, www.maxi-cosi.com
The Great Little Trading Company	www.gltc.co.uk
Halfords	www.halfords.com
Huggababy	www.huggababy.co.uk
Ikea	www.ikea.co.uk
John Lewis	www.johnlewis.com
JoJo Maman Bébé	www.jojomamanbebe.co.uk
Kids on the Move	www.kidsonthemove.co.uk
Krucial Kids	www.krucialkids.com
Lilliput	www.lilliput.com
Mothercare	www.mothercare.co.uk
Real Cycles	www.realcycles.com
Travelling with Children	www.travellingwithchildren.co.uk
Urchin	www.urchin.co.uk
Wilkinet	www.wilkinet.co.uk

Travelling checklist

Item	Notes
Car seat	
Car 'survival kit'	
Seat-belt accessories	
Sunblind	
Sleep cushion	
Rear-view mirror	
Fleece/car-seat cover	
Car bottle warmer	
Car tidy	
Car entertainment	
Baby carrier/sling	
Travel highchair	
Travel cot	
Bicycle seat	
Changing bag	
Sun protection	
Swim nappies/ buoyancy aids	
Other	

Chapter 6

First set of wheels

A pushchair or pram is likely to be one of the more expensive items you buy for your baby, but you don't need to spend an awful lot to get a decent one. Buying a pushchair is a bit like buying a car – any new car will get you there in reasonable comfort, but you will pay more for something with good suspension, luxury padded seating and fashionable styling. Perfectly acceptable buggy-style pushchairs, suitable from birth, can be found in nursery stores such as Mothercare★ for around £50–70 (or even less if you're prepared to forgo certain features). Alternatively, you could easily spend £300–500 on a top-of-the-range two-in-one or three-in-one (see page 175) pushchair, or a fashionable three-wheeler. There are many varieties of pushchair, and the pros and cons of the main different types are covered in this chapter. Your baby will probably be happy in whatever model you choose (as long as it's designed to be used from birth – see box overleaf) but your own needs are also very important. Before you buy you need to consider carefully the practicalities: some issues to think about are outlined below.

Questions to ask yourself before you buy

There is an element of compromise involved in buying any kind of pushchair. You are unlikely to find a pushchair that meets all your needs perfectly because all types have their advantages and disadvantages and your requirements may change too. However, by thinking carefully about factors such as where you live, how you plan to spend your days with your baby, whether you will be using public transport or how often you'll be using the car, and even how soon you plan to have another baby, you can help ensure that you buy a pushchair that serves you well. In order to help you decide what type would suit you, ask yourself the following questions.

Suitable from birth?

Ideally, newborns should lie flat for the first few months. Not all pushchairs recline enough to enable your baby to do this so, when you are choosing a pushchair for a new baby, you need to make sure the seat can fully recline. New babies need the back support that only a fully reclining pushchair can give. The manufacturer should make it clear on the information accompanying the pushchair whether or not it is suitable for use from birth. If in doubt, ask the retailer.

Until your baby is about three or four months old you should still be careful about back support, and babies should not sit in a pushchair that doesn't have any sort of recline until they are six months or so (i.e. until they can sit up). Even at this age some recline facility is still better, if the pushchair is being used regularly, to enable your baby to sleep comfortably.

- **Where will you be walking with your baby?** The kind of wheels a pushchair has will influence how easy it is to push across certain types of ground. Large, fixed wheels are better than smaller ones over rough or soft ground, so if you need regularly to go over grass or other unsealed surfaces to get to your house or walk in your park, larger wheels are better. Air-filled wheels (as are common to three-wheelers) will provide an even more comfortable ride. Smaller swivel wheels are best for around town, although these also need to be lockable so you can go over rougher ground too.

- **Do you want your baby to face you as you are pushing?** Many parents like to be able to look at their baby's face as they are pushing. This is not critical, of course, but when babies are very young their parents' faces are the most interesting and reassuring part of their world, and your baby will enjoy seeing you making faces at him or her as you walk along. Before too long, however, your baby will probably be more interested in viewing the surroundings and facing you won't be so important. A two-in-one or three-in-one pushchair that faces you when used as a pram but can be forward- or rearward-facing when used as a pushchair may suit your needs best.

- **Are there steps to your front door?** If so, a pram-style chassis (e.g. a two-in-one or three-in-one pushchair) may be too cumbersome to get up the steps smoothly, and you will end up hauling your sleeping baby awkwardly up the steps. You may well benefit from choosing a smaller, more lightweight option.

- **Where will you be keeping the pushchair when it's not in use?** Decide where, ideally, you would like to store the pushchair and make sure the model you want is suitable. Don't fool yourself into thinking you'll be folding the pushchair when it's not in use – realistically this is unlikely to happen, and you need to think of the pushchair in terms of its unfolded size, taking up space in the hallway. If you have a narrow hallway or other storage area, a bulky two-in-one or three-in-one may not be suitable for you.

- **Will you be using public transport on a regular basis?** If so, a lightweight, easy-folding pushchair or buggy that can be used from birth is what you need – bear in mind that you will probably have the baby under one arm while you fold the pushchair, so you should buy one with a folding mechanism that you can operate with one hand or foot. Fortunately lots of buses these days allow you to walk on with the pushchair unfolded.

- **Will you regularly be taking the pushchair with you in the car?** If your car boot is on the small side you'll need to check that the folded pushchair will fit into it. It is worth looking at the lighter, buggy-style options if you want to make lifting the pushchair in and out of the boot and folding and unfolding it as simple a task as possible. A 'travel system' pushchair will incur less risk of waking your baby up, because you can attach the car seat, complete with sleeping baby, straight on to the pushchair chassis.

- **How long will you be using the pushchair for?** A mistake many parents make is to buy a smart and pricey two-in-one, for example, then decide after a few months that a lightweight buggy will suit their needs much better. The two-in-one just ends up taking up space in the hall. In practical terms, it's only worth paying for a two-in-one or three-in-one if you are sure you will be using it over a couple of years or so. This is something hard to predict – but if you imagine yourself using the car a lot, visiting friends' houses, doing the shopping and fitting in strolls in the park, it's worth considering the advantages of a buggy-style pushchair. If you are planning to have another baby fairly soon after the first (say, within 18 months or so), then using a lightweight buggy for the toddler and a sling for the baby, or a double buggy for both, will be the easiest way of getting around.

- **Will you be putting your baby to sleep in the pushchair during the day?** If you expect that your baby will be using the pushchair instead of the cot for lengthy daytime naps, or you envisage whole afternoons in the park as a regular part of your routine with your new baby, a two-in-one or a three-in-one that comes with a carry cot and mattress is worth considering, as the most comfortable option for your baby's back. You can use a sheet and blankets with the carry cot on a three-in-one, while with a lie-back pushchair or a two-in-one, your baby is likely to be lying directly on the pushchair fabric. A traditional pram is also good for daytime naps although it is much less versatile in other respects.

- **Will you be using the pushchair to carry your shopping?** Shopping-basket capacity varies widely between pushchair types. If you are likely to be using the pushchair to help you carry more shopping than a pint of milk and a loaf of bread, look at the size of the shopping basket (if there is one) with a couple of bags of shopping in mind.

- **Would you consider buying more than one pushchair?** This can be the best option for many people as one type of pushchair may not suit all their requirements. You could, for example, have a two-in-one or three-in-one for daily use but also have a cheaper buggy for taking on holiday, for days out using the car or for using on public transport. You can buy a basic buggy, marketed as being suitable for a newborn baby, for as little as £20 or so. It won't be the most luxurious option for your baby but may be the most practical option for you.

- **How comfortable is it for you as well as your baby?** Your baby is likely to be fine in almost anything. Whether you will be comfortable pushing it is another matter. Handle height is critical: if you or your partner are taller than average you don't want to be stooping to push your baby – check out the feel of the handle height in the shop or make sure the handles are adjustable. Handles with a soft, rounded edge are kindest on the hands.

Types of pushchair

There are myriad styles of pushchair to choose from. The following categorisation covers all the main types.

Two-in-ones and three-in-ones

If you like the idea of your new baby being in a pram but want a pushchair for when he or she is a bit older, a two-in-one or three-in-one pram/pushchair combination could be a good choice. A two-in-one is a pushchair on a pram-like chassis, which can be used as an enclosed pram when fully reclined, or – with a few straightforward adjustments – as a pushchair. A three-in-one is the same but also comprises a carry cot, which you can put on the chassis or use as a separate sleeping place for naps or night-time sleeping before your baby moves into a cot (see Chapter 3 for more about sleeping options). Both come with a removable hood, apron and bumper bar (for when you are using it as a pushchair). Expect to pay around £260–350 for a two-in-one and £300–480 for a three-in-one. Accessories such as foot-muffs and rain covers (see pages 186–8) are sometimes included but more often are charged for separately.

Pros:
- ✔ pram-style chassis will usually have better suspension than that of a standard buggy-style pushchair – this makes for a more comfortable ride
- ✔ seats are normally both rearward- and forward-facing, so you can have your baby facing you when he or she is very young and facing forward when older
- ✔ many have fairly large, fixed wheels, which give a smoother ride, especially over rough ground
- ✔ useful if you want to use a pushchair for daytime sleeps at home – especially three-in-ones with their carry-cot option. (Some three-in-one carry cots come with a mattress; some don't. If you want to use the carry cot for night-time sleeping, you need to check the mattress is appropriate – the manufacturer should specify if it is suitable for night-time use. If one doesn't come as part of the basic price, expect to pay another £10–25 for a night-time mattress)
- ✔ shopping-basket area is usually a reasonable size.

Cons:

✘ their comparative bulk and weight can make these pushchairs feel cumbersome and they can be an obstruction at times

✘ large, fixed wheels are not as easy to manoeuvre (in and out of shops, up and down kerbs and around corners) as smaller, swivel wheels

✘ you may find you use the pram option a lot but, by the time you move on to the pushchair, the attractions of a lighter, more compact buggy-style pushchair may mean you end up buying one of these instead

✘ they are not a very portable option – although they fold, they . can still be heavy, take up quite a lot of space and may not fit in smaller car boots.

> ❝I felt under pressure in the shop to buy a three-in-one. The sales assistant plugged it as being really versatile so we ended up buying it. But we hardly used the carry cot – Jamie was sleeping in a crib that was given to us and I just used the pushchair in the lie-back position to go out.❞
>
> Susan, mother of Jamie, 8 months

> ❝We paid £350 for a very good-looking two-in-one pram/pushchair combo but only used it for three or four months. We were going on holiday, bought a buggy to take with us and never went back to the two-in-one – it just seemed so much more of a hassle.❞
>
> Kate, mother of Daisy, 14 months

Travel systems

These combine a baby car seat with a pushchair. Both the car seat and the pushchair seat are suitable for use from birth – the pushchair reclines fully and the car seat is an infant type (for more on car seats see pages 136–46). They cost between £120 and £380.

Pros:
- ✔ your baby can stay in the car seat to be moved from the car to the pushchair so there is less risk of waking him or her up
- ✔ buying the pushchair and car seat in one go means less time spent looking at all the different models of each
- ✔ useful if you also need to use public transport in the early days – you won't have to bundle your baby out of the pushchair to get on the bus. As long as you are using the car seat directly on the chassis, you can simply lift it out, rest your baby on the floor in the seat, fold the pushchair and walk on with car seat and folded pushchair under either arm (although no one could claim that this won't be heavy work)
- ✔ the car seat is rearward-facing on the pushchair, so your baby will be facing you as you are walking along
- ✔ if you will be using the car a lot, a travel system is probably your most convenient option.

Cons:
- ✘ you need to be absolutely sure the car seat fits your car properly before you buy, as not all models fit every type of car
- ✘ you must be wary of using the car seat as a pushchair seat too much: young babies' backs need to be well supported (see 'Suitable from birth?' box, page 172), and this is something the pushchair itself is designed for rather than the car seat. You should aim to limit pushing your baby around in the car seat to a couple of hours at the most
- ✘ bear in mind that you will need to buy another car seat within nine months or so, as the car seats to be used with these pushchairs are only for young babies – combination car seats (see pages 138 and 139) can be used by babies and older children, and you may decide that one of these and a separate pushchair might suit your needs better
- ✘ on some models, fitting the car seat to the chassis can be quite awkward and the instructions poor – try out a few models in the shop before you buy to make sure you are happy with the fitting technique.

Forward-facing pushchairs

These can be a good compromise if you want a lighter option than a two-in-one or three-in-one pram/pushchair combination. These pushchairs can be adjusted to lie flat for a newborn baby (they usually have a choice of three or four recline positions) and are designed so there is adequate padding and back support to keep your baby comfortable. They are often buggy-like (see below) in style but tend to be wider and often have larger, swivel wheels. Like buggies, some have 'umbrella folding'. Others fold flat. Retailers usually recommend that you buy a footmuff (see 'Pushchair accessories', on pages 185–188) to go with these pushchairs so that your baby can be enclosed for extra warmth.

Pros:

✔ a more lightweight, less bulky and easier-to-fold alternative to a two-in-one or three-in-one

✔ often have more storage space for shopping than buggies

✔ take up less space than a two- or three-in-one, so useful if you have a small hallway or if you will regularly be visiting friends' houses with limited space

✔ generally cheaper than pram/pushchair combinations – models are priced from about £50 to £250, and there is a reasonable choice around the £100 mark.

Cons:

✘ your baby may be more exposed than in a pram/pushchair combination, so you will need to be more vigilant when wrapping him or her up

✘ forward-facing, so you won't be able to see your baby's face as clearly as with a pushchair in the 'facing towards you' position when you are walking along (although some have a 'window' in the hood).

Three-wheelers

Not so long ago, pushing a three-wheeler got you quizzical looks from passers-by. Today, three-wheelers are regarded by many as the most stylish pushchair they can buy. Originally designed to appeal to fitness enthusiasts and serious walkers who had started families but were still keen to pursue their training and interests, three-wheelers are now just as common a sight in the supermarket or the local park as on a hillside path. The basic design of a three-wheeler is a triangular-shaped chassis with an aluminium or steel frame and a fabric, weatherproof seat, on top of three fairly large, pneumatic tyre wheels. The idea is that they enable you to push your baby relatively smoothly over all kinds of terrain, from a beach to a muddy footpath to a pavement, with the tyres rather than your baby absorbing the bumps. Although to a novice the different makes may all look more or less the same, you'll find that prices vary widely. Top-of-the-range three-wheelers can reach the £400 price mark; you can also get perfectly good three-wheelers for less than £100. If you prefer the idea of your new baby being in a completely flat, pram-style enclosure, you can get three-wheelers with a carry-cot attachment. You can also get 'travel system' three-wheelers.

Pros:

✔ if you are keen on the outdoor life, especially if you enjoy walking, a good three-wheeler will enable you go to places with your baby that would be uncomfortable and difficult with a standard pushchair

✔ those with a front swivel wheel (not all have these) can be easier to handle than bulkier pram/pushchair combinations in urban environments as well as in the countryside

✔ some models are incredibly light – these will have an aluminium frame and are likely to be at the pricier end of the market

✔ if you like the idea of jogging with your pushchair, you can buy three-wheelers specially suited to this – you need to choose one with large wheels (with some models there is a choice of wheel size), a back axle that won't get in your way, a handbrake to control speed and a hand strap for extra security

✔ you don't need to pay over the odds for a decent three-wheeler – in *Which?* tests in 2002, two Mothercare★ models, the Urban Detour Glacier (now £160) and the Urban Detour Arctic (now £100) were both recommended as Best Buys.

Cons:

✘ it is easy to be swayed by fashion, but *Which?* research has shown that three-wheelers have no advantage over four wheels for normal use around town, and that if you're unlikely to be using the pushchair over rough surfaces it's best to go for a conventional model – think about your daily needs rather than the label or style of a pushchair before you buy

✗ although many models fold easily these aren't as compact when folded as many buggies – you can normally take the wheels off, which makes storage in the car boot easier, but they still aren't the quickest pushchair to get up and going once you get them out

✗ their longer shape means they can be harder to manoeuvre in confined spaces than standard (forward-facing) pushchairs

✗ pneumatic tyres may make the ride smoother but they can also puncture – you'll need to take a puncture repair kit out with you if you want to be fully prepared.

>❝My three-wheeler pushchair has fantastic suspension and gives the baby a very comfy ride – but it's impossible to steer and takes a huge effort to fold away. If your heart is set on a three-wheeler, make sure you choose one with a swivel front wheel.❞
>
> Kate, mother of Silas, 13 months

>❝I admit that we went for a three-wheeler mainly because we thought they looked good, but we've been really pleased with it – I never thought I'd be doing so much walking before I had a baby and I know I can just about go anywhere with this.❞
>
> Ian, father of Meg, 5 months

Safety watch

If you are planning to use your three-wheeler over rough ground, bear in mind that you shouldn't really do this until your baby is about six months old, as until this age babies' necks are not strong enough to take the strain of a bouncing head.

Buggies or strollers

These are lightweight pushchairs that fold up quickly and easily into a relatively flat shape ('umbrella folding'). Many are for babies of around three to four months and over, as they do not provide sufficient back support for younger babies, although some models can be used from birth. Some models don't recline at all and these shouldn't be used until your baby is six to nine months old. Some come with more features than others – for example, a multi-position seat, removable washable covers or an inclusive rain cover and hood – and the price you pay will reflect this. You can pay as little as £20 or so for the simplest model, with more sophisticated models reaching the £100 mark.

Pros:

✔ the most versatile type of pushchair for older babies and toddlers – their weight and ease of folding means you can take them just about anywhere, and they are particularly suited to walking round the shops or going on public transport

✔ many models are relatively inexpensive (compared with pram/pushchair combinations) – you can buy a perfectly acceptable mid-range stroller with all the most useful features for £50–70

✔ popular with toddlers as they feel less 'hemmed in'

✔ small, swivel wheels common to these pushchairs make them especially suitable for city and town streets.

Cons:

✘ the simplest, cheapest models do lack features that are likely to be useful, such as lockable swivel wheels and comfortable handles, so aren't the best for daily use – decide which features you think you will need before you choose your model

✘ the weight varies between different models and this won't necessarily be related to price – some of these supposedly lightweight pushchairs can be quite heavy to push. Try them out before you buy

✘ they don't have the suspension of many other pushchairs and the ride won't be as smooth (although this isn't likely to bother your toddler)

✘ they tend to lack decent-sized shopping storage space – check this out if it is likely to be important to you.

> **"**We were on a fairly tight budget and bought a fully reclining buggy-style pushchair in a sale for about £70. It has been fine for two babies – the only drawback is I did feel they were a bit exposed in it when they were tiny but I just used to make sure they were wrapped up.**"**
>
> Alice, mother of Nathan, 4, and Ruby, 2

Buying tip

Prams and pushchairs are subject to fashion and manufacturers regularly change the patterns and designs of the materials used. This means that 'last season's' designs are often available at sale prices.

Other types of pushchair and pram

If you're after something a bit different, there are always new styles coming on to the market. The success of three-wheelers has spurred manufacturers into developing more adventurous designs that may appeal to some parents. For example, new on the market in 2004 is the Xplory by Stokke★. The 'chassis' of this pushchair is raised much higher off the ground than with a normal pushchair, the idea being that your baby is raised above the level of traffic fumes and general pavement grime. It's designed for urban living and because of its height can also double up as a highchair when you're out. At £499, though, it's at the pricey end of the market. The Bugaboo Frog is another new-style pushchair. It has two small buggy-sized wheels and two much larger wheels. You can reverse the handlebars so that you have the large wheels at the front or the back depending on the terrain. The small wheels can also be folded up so that the larger wheels can take the strain on their own – useful for pulling the pushchair on a beach or in the snow. Again, at £499, these are an expensive option, and, at the time of writing, is not widely available – try the Lullabys★ website if you're interested.

If you really want to get noticed, you could get a traditional 'Mary Poppins'-style metal-chassis pram. These are comfy and enclosed for your baby, and the large wheels ensure a smooth ride. You can't fold up the most traditional models and they take up a large amount of space in the hallway. Although they don't really fit in with modern lifestyles, they are quite special-looking. Silver Cross is the main brand, available from John Lewis★, and selected independent nursery retailers (you can check local availability on the Silver Cross★ website). The prams are just about as pricey as you can get, at around £700–800.

Double pushchairs

If you are having twins or you have a young toddler and are expecting a baby, a double pushchair will probably be high up on your shopping list. The basic choice is between a side-by-side or a tandem style. Side-by-side pushchairs are usually suitable for twins from birth as well as for an older child and a baby. Tandem pushchairs tend to be suitable for a toddler and a baby, or two older babies, as usually only the back seat is fully reclining. You can get two-in-one, three-in-one and three-wheeler versions of side-by-side pushchairs. There is less variety with tandem pushchairs.

With double pushchairs, more than with any other type, what is best for you depends on your own circumstances and preferences, and you may have to compromise on one feature at the expense of another – for example, if you want a side-by-side with reasonably roomy seats you'll have to go for a wider model that won't fit as easily through many doorways.

Bear in mind that there are alternatives to double pushchairs – not so much for twins, but if you have a toddler and a baby, a sling and a light buggy, or a pushchair and some sort of toddler platform (see 'Pushchair accessories' on pages 185 and 186) may be a better choice for you.

Side-by-side pushchairs

Pros:

✔ tend to be more compact and portable than tandems
✔ generally the most lightweight choice, although weight can vary hugely between models (some models are under 8kg, others weigh almost 20kg) – if weight is important to you, check the label
✔ fairly small, swivel wheels common to many side-by-side pushchairs are useful for manoeuvring around town

✔ usually suitable for twins from birth as well as for a newborn and a toddler

✔ you can buy three-wheeler versions if you like the advantages of these (see pages 178–80) – although these are the most expensive option (Mothercare's★ cheapest side-by-side standard pushchair costs £100 and the cheapest three-wheeler version £200).

Cons:

✘ can be more difficult to get through doorways than tandems

✘ access to shopping basket may be tricky when seats are reclined

✘ on some models, the choice is between either fully upright or fully reclined seating, with no intermediate options – those with semi-recline as well are more flexible.

Tandem pushchairs
Pros:

✔ compact shape width-wise means they are easier to manoeuvre through doorways

✔ sturdier feel than many buggy-style, side-by-side pushchairs

✔ tandem style makes it more difficult for an older child to harass a baby (although, in later months, the child seated in the back may enjoy pulling the hair of the child in front).

Cons:

✘ rear seat often has limited leg room so can be restrictive for an older baby

✘ usually little head support in the front seat for a toddler who falls asleep

✘ unless there are two hoods, some tandem models don't offer much weather protection for the child in the front seat

✘ more bulky and cumbersome to fold than side-by-side pushchairs

✘ not as widely available as side-by-side pushchairs and less choice of styles.

Buying second-hand

Pushchairs and prams are often bought second-hand or passed on between family or friends. If you will be using a second-hand pushchair, check for the following:

- properly working brakes
- correctly aligned wheels
- all folding parts operating smoothly
- two locking mechanisms working efficiently and safely (this is to ensure that the pushchair doesn't fold up or collapse while a child is in it)
- no rust
- fabric in reasonably good condition and not weakened by any tears
- handles and frame with no unusual-looking bends or kinks
- a five-point rather than a three-point harness; this is safer and conforms to current safety standards.

Manufacturers are usually willing to service and repair second-hand pushchairs and check that they conform to safety requirements.

Pushchair accessories

Of course, you don't have to stop at buying the pushchair. Pushchair manufacturers and others have come up with a range of accessories designed for your or your baby's convenience or comfort. Bear in mind that some extras can add substantially to the cost of the basic pushchair – for example, a rain cover, footmuff and sun canopy for a two-in-one could, depending on the manufacturer, set you back an extra £80–90 on top of the £350 or so you may have already paid for the pushchair.

Toddler platforms

If you have a baby and an older child and you only want one pushchair in use at one time, a toddler platform can make your life easier. (These are often known as 'buggy boards', a brand name of a main manufacturer.) You fit the wheeled platform on to your pram

> ### *Buying tip*
> *When you look at the price of a pushchair or buggy in the shop, check whether it includes a rain cover – some models do; some don't. You can only make meaningful price comparisons once you know what is included in the display price.*

or pushchair (you'll need to buy the right sort as they differ depending on what kind of pram or pushchair you have) and your toddler or pre-schooler can hop on when he or she doesn't want to walk. It is hard to predict before you buy how much use you will get out of one of these. If your older child seems to enjoy walking and doesn't tend to moan about wanting to go in the pushchair, you can easily get by without one. Many parents who opt to buy one do find them useful, however, if only for a few months while their older child builds up his or her walking stamina. They can also be useful for getting from A to B quickly without having to chivvy a dawdling three-year-old to keep up. Toddler platforms cost around £40 and are available from selected nursery stores or by mail order from a range of companies including Cheeky Rascals★, The Great Little Trading Company★ and the Boots★ website.

Footmuffs

Retailers and manufacturers often recommend you buy one of these to go with your new pushchair, if one isn't already included. It is a sort of 'bottom-half' sleeping bag, which helps keep your baby warm and offers some protection against the elements. Footmuffs are not essential and many parents are happy to keep their baby warm with blankets and appropriate clothing, but they can make keeping your baby snug a bit easier. They cost around £30–45.

Buggy weights

It's very tempting to hang shopping bags on the back of a buggy but if your toddler gets out, buggy and shopping end up overturned on the floor. It is also possible for a pushchair to 'up-end' with your baby in it if the bags are particularly heavy. Buggy weights are designed to be attached to the base of a buggy and provide enough ballast to hang a fair amount of shopping from the handles without the risk of your buggy up-ending. Because they are attached to both front wheels the extra weight is evenly distributed so doesn't make a significant difference to the ease of pushing. The weights are easily removable for when you're not shopping and could be worth a try if you regularly use your buggy as a shopping-bag carrier. They are available from Cheeky Rascals★ for £10.

Changing bags
Many pushchair manufacturers produce changing bags to coordinate with the design of their pushchair fabrics. If you like the idea of everything matching you may decide a coordinating bag is for you, but bear in mind that other changing bags could be worth a look and might be more suitable for your needs. For more on changing bags see pages 164 and 165.

Sun canopies and parasols
These are widely available and can help to shade your baby on sunny days – but they are often ineffective on their own simply because the sun and the pushchair will be changing positions as you walk and as the day goes on. Parasols in particular need to be regularly adjusted, can be fiddly and may end up being simply annoying. To be sure of sun protection when using a parasol or canopy, make sure exposed areas of your baby's skin are covered with a high-protection children's sun cream and that he or she is wearing a sun hat (see pages 166 and 167 for more about sun protection). Expect to pay about £10–30.

Rain covers
A decent rain cover will certainly protect your baby from the elements, but they can be a hassle to fold, unfold and fit in the first place, as well as being a moderately expensive extra (expect to pay £30-plus for a rain cover for a two-in-one pushchair). Some parents can't imagine being without one while others barely, if ever, use one. If you usually have a car at hand or if you live in a town and can easily nip into a café or shop doorway when there is a downpour, the value of a rain cover diminishes. Bear in mind that a few drops of rain aren't going to harm your baby, especially if he or she is protected by clothing and perhaps a pram or pushchair hood anyway. Older babies and toddlers may fight against having the rain cover put on and many parents give up altogether, especially if the rain doesn't seem particularly bad.

The most effective rain covers, should you choose to buy one, are 'all-in-one' and give your baby ample room to wave about or kick his or her legs without feeling claustrophobic. You can also buy showerproof covers for under £10 – these are elasticated pieces of showerproof fabric that you fit loosely over a pushchair, with a gap for your baby's head. They are very light so can be folded and kept in a bag for emergencies, and can be useful if you want some level of rain protection but don't want a full rain cover.

> **"I think rain covers are good if it's just a particularly blustery day, for keeping the baby out of the wind."**
>
> Kate, mother of Silas, 13 months

Insect and cat nets

If you plan to have your baby napping in the pram in the garden during the summer months, insect and cat nets, which fit over the whole body of the pram, can give you a bit more peace of mind. Pram cat nets are available from nursery stores and cost about £4–5.

Pushchair toys

There is a wide range of toys available that you can attach to the pushchair so your baby can play without the toy falling out of reach. These range from rattles and soft toys to relatively elaborate play devices that fit across the pushchair so your baby can press and tweak all manner of buttons and knobs. Bear in mind that, whatever the toy, the more your baby sees it the less novel it will be, so if you can, try to change pushchair toys fairly regularly.

Websites

Boots	www.boots.com
Cheeky Rascals	www.cheekyrascals.co.uk
The Great Little Trading Company	www.gltc.co.uk
John Lewis	www.johnlewis.com
Lullabys	www.lullabys.co.uk
Mothercare	www.mothercare.co.uk
Silver Cross	www.silvercross.co.uk
Stokke	www.stokke.com

Pushchair checklist

Pushchair	Notes
Two-in-one	
Three-in-one	
Travel system	
Forward-facing	
Three-wheeler	
Buggy/stroller	
Traditional pram	
Side-by-side	
Tandem	
Accessory	
Toddler platform	
Footmuff	
Buggy weights	
Changing bag (Ch 5)	
Sun canopy/parasol	
Rain cover	
Insect/cat net	
Pushchair toys	

Chapter 7

Safety devices

Each year, about 600,000 children aged under five are injured in the home badly enough to go to hospital. You can help prevent your child from joining these statistics by being vigilant around the potential accident hot-spots in your home.

Your young baby is relatively safe in your home. He or she can't move around independently so isn't likely to get into danger. Toddlers are a different matter: they will inevitably fall and trip in their uncoordinated efforts to explore. They don't understand the concept of danger so may ignore or forget your warnings about what they should or shouldn't do. Although you may watch them as much as you can, there are bound to be moments when they are out of your sight, particularly if, say, you are attending to a new baby.

A wide range of child safety gadgets is available from nursery and high-street stores. Many of these are very simple and cost just a few pounds – for example, corner guards for tables are £2 for a pack of four, and door slam stoppers, which protect little fingers, cost about £3 for two. You can also buy safety 'starter packs', containing a selection of such devices, for less than £10. Protection for your child from many household injuries can therefore be bought fairly cheaply. However, no home can be entirely child-proof. Most safety gadgets present some level of inconvenience to adults, so even if you have them you may be tempted not to use them all the time. Neither are they effective for all age groups – overcoming them depends on the skills level that children have reached, and if there are older children in the house you have to try to make sure they don't leave cupboards, gates and doors open. So even with the extra protection afforded by these products, you still need to be vigilant.

The Child Accident Prevention Trust★, a charity that educates and campaigns on safety issues relating to children, has a range of free leaflets on different aspects of baby and child safety for which you can send off (enclose a stamped addressed envelope). You can also download a selection of safety factsheets from its website.

Safety gadgets room by room

Living room

Most accidents happen in the living room, mainly because this is where most family activity takes place. Devices to consider include the following.

- **Fireguard** – if you have any sort of fire, a fireguard is a must. It needs to be full size and hooked to the wall for maximum safety. A proper fireguard should also have a top that prevents items from being thrown into the fire – a curved top is best because this is also a deterrent against placing objects on it. A simple spark guard or fire screen (which is a smaller guard designed to offer protection against sparks from an open fire, and is positioned much closer to the fire with minimal 'overhead' protection and not secured to the wall) is not sufficient to protect your child. Fireguards are widely available from nursery stores and catalogues – expect to pay £20–25. You can also buy **radiator guards** if you are worried about your child burning him- or herself on a hot radiator. Try one of the larger DIY stores or check out Rad Pad radiator covers, from around £30 depending on size and available from Baby Echoes★.
- **Corner guards** – these are plastic corner covers to help protect babies and toddlers from bumps against low tables and shelves. They are widely available and cheap.
- **Door slam stoppers** – these prevent doors from shutting on small fingers and also stop children from shutting themselves in a room. Some types of stopper prevent fingers from getting trapped in one side of the door but not the other – for example, the hinge side might be protected but the door can still be closed. If you want maximum protection, choose a stopper designed to protect both sides – try the Baby Dan★ Finger Safe or use a door stop to prevent the door from moving at all. You can also buy stoppers designed for sliding patio doors.

- **Glass safety film** – if you are fitting new glass in your home (for example, glass doors to your patio), they will need to be made of safety glass. (The characteristics of safety glass depend on the type – for example, toughened glass breaks into blunt shapes rather than sharp shards while laminated glass will 'craze' but won't actually crack.) If you have existing doors that aren't made of safety glass you can cover the glass with safety film, which will contain any jagged shards should the glass break. You can also use this for glass-topped tables. It is widely available, including from Mothercare★.
- **Socket covers** – electricity isn't a major contributor to child accident statistics but many parents feel reassured by having socket covers in place. Choose plain, simple ones – you want to make the socket area boring rather than inviting. A better option than buying covers for every socket is to protect your house's wiring with a residual current device (RCD). This is basically an electricity 'cut-out' device, which protects against electrocution by automatically cutting the electricity supply within a fraction of a second if it detects a fault or an unusual surge.
- **Video lock** – little fingers just can't seem to stay away from the video slot. A simple video lock covers the slot so your child can't shove fingers or small objects in. This is useful as a video-repair prevention device as much as a mechanism to prevent your child's fingers getting trapped. They are widely available.
- **Playpen** – if you need to leave a crawling baby or young toddler alone in a room for a short while, perhaps to answer the door or telephone, a playpen can be a useful 'security zone' in which to place him or her. See pages 205–7 for more about playpens.
- **Toy box** – although not a safety device as such, it is a good idea to have a box in your living room if many of your child's toys accumulate in there. Toys left on the floor are a tripping hazard, and a handy box for you to throw everything in when you get the chance is a good preventive measure. Make sure you get one with a slow-closing hinge so that little fingers can't get bruised by a slamming lid.

Safety watch

Hot drinks on low tables or the arms of chairs can cause serious burns to babies and toddlers. Bear in mind that a cup of tea or coffee can be hot enough to burn for as long as 20 minutes after it has been made.

Kitchen

The kitchen is full of potential dangers. Obvious ones are burns and scalds from kettles, pans and cookers; swallowing or touching dangerous fluids; or injury from kitchen implements. Gadgets to prevent these accidents include the following.

- **Cupboard and drawer catches** – these are designed to allow a cupboard or drawer to be opened only a few centimetres unless an adult releases the catch. Children will eventually learn how to operate them, but in the meantime they can provide a degree of reassurance. Catches are easy to fit and are usually opened by depressing the latch with a finger while opening the door or drawer.
- **Hob guard** – these can help prevent young children reaching up to hot surfaces or pulling on cooking pot handles. They are widely available, from nursery stores and other shops that sell safety products, and cost about £10–15. However, they aren't necessarily a good idea. Some guards can get hot enough to cause burns themselves, and some have bars that children's fingers can get through. Also, you need to lift a pan over a hob guard, which could in itself cause an accident.
- **Gate or barrier** – the best way of preventing your child from the dangers of the kitchen is to try to keep him or her out of there as much as possible. A gate or barrier (see page 195) is the best way of doing this, as your child can still watch you when you are in the kitchen but will be out of harm's way.
- **Fridge guard/lock** – this is a simple catch that you attach to the side of the fridge. The fridge surface to which you attach it needs to be clean and grease-free, otherwise the guard can be easily pulled off. Available from nursery stores or other safety product outlets.

- **Curly flex** – a curly flex on a kettle can help prevent your child from pulling boiling water over him- or herself.

Safety watch
When cooking, use the back burners or hotplates whenever possible, and turn the pan handles towards the back. Keep the kettle to the back of the work surface, out of children's reach at all times. Water is still hot enough to scald for at least 20 minutes after boiling.

Stairs
Crawling babies and toddlers can sustain serious injuries falling down the stairs. It is worth making the stairs inaccessible to them until they are steady on their feet and more aware of the dangers. There are a couple of devices you can use to protect them.

- **Barriers and gates** – these are usually meant only for children up to about two years old (three- and four-year-olds will probably be capable of opening them). Ideally you need two barriers or gates – one at the top of the stairs and one at the bottom. Many gates have a low bar across the bottom, which makes them more stable. However, adults could trip over this bar when they are going through the gate at the top of the stairs, so you need to be extra careful with these (although, depending on the brand of gate, you may be able to buy an anti-trip attachment). Rigid, fixed barriers are more awkward to negotiate than gates if you need to move around the house in a hurry. You can also buy fabric barriers that roll back when not in use so they are less obtrusive. Whether you choose a barrier or a gate, ideally you should be able to open it with one hand as you may be carrying a child.

Hallway and landing
One essential safety device you should not be without is a **smoke alarm.** You should have these in your house anyway, but having children often galvanises people into installing smoke alarms if they haven't done so before. If you live in a flat or bungalow, one alarm

---

Safety watch

Barriers and gates will not be effective if they are badly fitted or if the surfaces to which you attach them aren't sound, so check for wobbly banisters and suspect plaster that could give way under pressure.

---

should be enough in the hallway. If your home has more than one floor, put one alarm at the bottom of the stairs and one on each upstairs landing. Test the alarms at least every month to make sure they are operating correctly and replace the batteries every year. Expect to pay from £5 for a standard smoke alarm.

Bathroom

The key dangers to children in a bathroom are drowning in the bath water and poisoning from medicines and toxic cleaners that haven't been safely stored away. Other risks include slipping on wet surfaces and scalding from hot water. Devices to consider include the following.

- **Medicine cabinet** – one that you can lock is best, even if you think the cabinet is out of your child's reach. Before too long he or she will be moving chairs or clothes baskets around to use as a platform to stand on.
- **Bath thermometer** – if you are anxious about the temperature of your baby's bath, you can buy a bath thermometer to accurately test the water. These are relatively inexpensive and are widely available. You can also buy bath mats and plugs that change colour when the water is too hot (Mothercare★ sells a Little Fish colour-change bath mat for £13).
- A more permanent solution is a **thermostatic mixing valve (TMV)**. TMVs are control devices that mix hot water from your boiler with your cold-water supply in such a way that the water coming out of your tap never exceeds a preset temperature. They have been used for several years in hospitals but new government proposals have been put forward recommending that by 2006 all newly built or converted homes should have TMVs fitted to wash basins, showers and baths. Each TMV will cost from about £50 but should dramatically

reduce the number of children who are scalded by bath water every year. At the time of writing, TMVs are not generally available from DIY stores and can only be bought from plumbing or building suppliers. The manufacturers also recommend that only a plumber should fit them.

- **Non-slip bath mat** – young children see the bath as a playground and will want to stand up and mess around, particularly if there is more than one of them in the bath. A simple bath mat will prevent your child from slipping on the base of the bath. For more on these see page 50.
- **Toilet seat lock** – this will prevent your child from opening the toilet lid and putting his or her hands inside the toilet.
- **Toilet steps and adaptors** – these can help children feel more secure and prevent them from falling off when they are learning to use the toilet (see pages 209 and 210 for more details).

Safety watch

Never leave a baby or a young child alone in or near a bath, even for a moment (say, if you have to nip to the phone or take something out of the oven). Accidents can happen in a few seconds and a baby can drown in 2.5cm of water.

Nursery

Falling out of an upstairs window is the most serious hazard presented by any upstairs room. As well as taking precautions against this you may want to consider fitting cupboard locks or door slam stoppers (see page 192) in the nursery if trapped fingers are a worry. Other safety products include the following.

- **Baby monitors** – these shouldn't really be regarded as a safety device. They are more for your convenience, so you can hear your child crying if you are in another part of the house or in the garden. But they can alert you to potential hazards such as your child climbing out of the cot. For more on baby monitors see pages 53–8.

- **Window locks** – most windows without a lock are potentially hazardous to a small child, but upstairs windows in the nursery or another bedroom are particularly worth making child-resistant. Some lock with a separate key (so you have to keep it somewhere accessible to you but not to your child); others are keyless and have a mechanism that requires you to do two actions at once (which should foil a small child). All allow the window to open a couple of centimetres when they're in use.
- **Bed guard** – this can help prevent your child from falling out of bed until he or she is used to being in a bed rather than a cot. You can choose from wooden grid-like styles or soft mesh styles with a rigid edge; they are priced from about £20. As long as you have one side of the bed against the wall, you'll only need one guard. Bear in mind that lots of children take to a bed very easily and rarely, if ever, fall out and that even if they do, a bump and a bit of a shock is all they're likely to get.

Safety watch

Keep furniture, including beds, away from windows, so that young children won't be able to climb on to them to get to the window.

First aid

You can buy ready-stocked first-aid kits from stores such as Boots★ and Superdrug, but if you want to be sure you have everything you might need it's worth putting together your own kit. All the items listed below should be available to buy separately from a well-stocked chemist. Keep your kit in a secure box out of your child's reach and check the contents regularly in case anything needs to be replaced. Make sure that other adults who may look after your child at your home know where your first-aid box is.

A well-stocked first-aid kit should contain:

- 1 small roller bandage
- 1 large roller bandage
- 1 small conforming bandage (these shape themselves to the body contours)

- scissors
- calamine cream
- pack of gauze swabs
- 2 triangular bandages (can be used as slings)
- hypoallergenic tape (for securing dressings)
- 2 sterile pads
- waterproof plasters
- 1 finger bandage and applicator
- tweezers
- 1 sterile dressing with bandage.

Various household items can also be used successfully in a first-aid emergency – for burns in particular. For example:

- a clean sheet or pillowcase can make an effective loose protective covering for burns
- plastic kitchen film can be used to dress burns
- a clean plastic bag can be secured around a burned hand or foot.

If you can, go on a first-aid course so you know how to use items such as bandages properly, or buy a first-aid book and keep it at hand (try *First Aid for Children Fast*, published by Dorling Kindersley, £9.99). For details of local first-aid courses, look under British Red Cross or St John's Ambulance (St Andrew's Ambulance in Scotland) in your telephone directory or Yellow Pages.

Websites

Baby Dan	www.babydan.com
Baby Echoes	www.babyechoes.co.uk
Boots	www.boots.com
Child Accident Prevention Trust	www.capt.org.uk
Mothercare	www.mothercare.co.uk

Safety devices checklist

Item	Notes
Fireguard	
Radiator guards	
Table/shelf corner guards	
Door slam stoppers	
Glass safety film	
Electric socket covers	
Video lock	
Playpen (Ch 8)	
Toy box	
Drawer/cupboard catches	
Hob guard	
Gates/barriers	
Fridge guard/lock	
Curly kettle flex	
Smoke alarms	
Medicine cabinet	
Bath thermometer	
Non-slip bath mat	
Toilet seat lock	
Toilet steps/adaptor (Ch 8)	
Baby monitor (Ch 2)	
Window locks	
Bed guard	
First-aid kit	
First-aid book	

Chapter 8

Growing up

Once your baby is strong enough to support his or her head, another world of entertainment possibilities is opened up. Apart from new and exciting toys (see Chapter 9), you can buy mobility products that can be fun for your baby and entertaining for you to watch.

Later on, once your baby reaches the age of two or so, toilet training will be firmly on the agenda. The process and completion of toilet training signifies the true end of babyhood for many parents – but bear in mind that most will be wiping bottoms for a few years to come yet!

Entertainment

Before your baby becomes fully mobile, baby bouncers and baby walkers offer the opportunity for new freedom and adventure. This is also a time when it could be useful to familiarise your baby with a playpen – it will provide you with a degree of control over those potentially hazardous early explorations when he or she begins crawling and walking.

Baby bouncers

Baby bouncers have a big 'wow' factor for many babies. They can be used from about four months of age – as soon as your baby can support his or her head. Your baby sits in a special seat that is attached to a long elasticated strip, the top of which you clamp to the doorframe, pushes against the floor with his or her feet, and bounces up and down. The bouncing sensation can delight babies (and be hilarious to watch) – it will probably be the first time your baby has felt the thrill of being able to move fast using his or her own leg muscles. However, even babies who love these bouncers may tire of them after ten minutes or so, and you should keep sessions fairly brief – 15 minutes is fine; 30 minutes the absolute limit. Not all babies like bouncing so it may be worth borrowing a bouncer to try out before you buy.

Types of bouncer

There are two types of baby bouncer – the main difference being between a simple, harness-style fabric seat or a seat with a moulded plastic surround, sometimes in the shape of a cartoon character or animal. Expect to pay about £20 for the fabric type (for example, the Lindam★ Bounce About for £20 from Mothercare★ or independent nursery stores, or the more padded Lindam 'bounce about plus' for £30) and £30–40 for the moulded plastic sort (such as the Tigger door bouncer, £40 from Mothercare★). Both types have their advantages and disadvantages (see below).

Whichever type of seat you choose, you need to make sure your doorframes and doorways are suitable for a bouncer. The frame must be sturdy and solid as it will need to take the weight of your baby. It should also be perfectly straight and the gap between the frame and the wall should be wide enough for the clamp to fit on to it properly. Most doorframes are fine but it is worth double-checking before you buy. Narrow doorways are not particularly suitable for bouncer use because your baby will be bouncing sideways as well as up and down, so he or she could knock against the frame.

Plastic-seat bouncers

Pros:

✔ provides protection against bumps on the doorframe
✔ wipes clean.

Cons:

✘ can be more constricting than the fabric type (and therefore possibly less fun for your baby)
✘ takes up space both to use and to store.

Fabric-seat bouncers

Pros:

✔ smaller seat gives a bit more freedom for your baby to move and flail arms about

✔ lightweight and easy to fold and store

✔ least expensive type.

Cons:

✘ provides less protection against knocks and may make your baby feel more vulnerable.

Baby walkers

A baby walker is basically a seat with a table within a wheeled metal frame. Your baby can sit in the walker and trundle about by pushing along with his or her feet. Despite the name, baby walkers are not designed to help a baby learn to walk – more to provide them with mobility and entertainment at a time when they might be starting to get frustrated at their inability to get about.

Many parents swear by the usefulness of baby walkers, especially for babies with lots of 'get up and go', but the products have also had a bad press. Safety experts would prefer that parents avoided baby walkers altogether. The main problem is that walkers may not be very stable when encountering an uneven surface, such as the edge of a carpet, and this, often combined with the fair speed at which some babies can 'drive' them, can make them prone to tipping over. As well as overturning on to the floor, walkers and their occupants can fall down stairs, roll against fires and heaters and tip into swimming pools. The majority of injuries are to the head and face. Walkers can also take you by surprise because they enable your baby to reach for things (in a low cupboard or on a low shelf, for example) that you may not be prepared for.

So if walkers are so widely regarded as dangerous, why would anyone want to buy one? The simple answer is that babies can have a lot of fun in them and they can considerably broaden the horizons of those who may have been getting frustrated with the same old routine. The danger really arises when parents or carers do not watch their charges while they are in the walker – the babies most likely to be hurt in walker accidents are those who are left in them while their parents' attention is elsewhere, even for a short time.

Manufacturers have come up with versions of traditional walkers that don't move as fast across the floor and are therefore somewhat safer. Mothercare★, for instance, has walkers with 'slo-go' wheels that restrict your baby's movement. Go for one of these if you like the idea of a walker but want to minimise the risks.

Pros:

✔ babies usually have fun using baby walkers

✔ wheels can be locked so that you can also use the walker as a feeding chair or, by putting toys on the tray, as a stationary 'play seat' (some walkers come with a play-tray attachment with built-in toys)

✔ they fold flat enough for you to store under a bed when not in use.

Cons:

✘ the potential hazards with the use of baby walkers are a real concern, so if you are planning to use one you do need to be vigilant

✘ their use may be limited to a fairly short developmental period – maybe only a few weeks – between sitting and crawling or walking, so you may decide the expense (around £25–50), and possibly the extra anxiety, isn't worth it

✘ there may be a temptation, if your baby really enjoys using the walker, to keep him or her in it for too long; but use should be limited to no more than 30 minutes at a time as your baby still needs the full range of movement at this stage of development.

A walker alternative

If you don't like the idea of a baby walker but would like your baby to have a new and potentially exciting play place in your home, you could think about a stationary baby 'play station' or 'static exercisers'. These have a similar design to baby walkers but don't have wheels – instead your baby sits and swivels around. Although they don't provide the same experience as a baby walker, the fun for your baby comes from pushing with his or her legs to spin the seating area round and rock to and fro. There is also generally a gadget-filled play tray with other toys around the rim. The Graco★ Fun

Safety watch

- *Never leave your baby unattended in a walker.*
- *Never let your baby use the walker near steps, stairs or thresholds.*
- *If possible, confine use of the walker to one room at a time, keeping doors shut.*
- *Check that surfaces are flat and free of objects that may cause tipping over.*
- *Be extra vigilant if allowing your baby to use the walker in the garden, especially as the surface – on a patio, for example – may be uneven.*
- *Check that both your baby's feet touch the floor – the seat height should be adjustable for this purpose.*
- *Never carry the walker with your baby in it.*
- *Avoid use near fires or stoves – and radiators, if possible.*
- *Always use the harness that comes with the walker.*
- *Stop using the walker when your baby reaches the maximum weight recommended by the manufacturer.*
- *Walkers are not suitable for babies who cannot support their heads or who are already accomplished walkers.*
- *Limit use to a maximum of 30 minutes at a time.*

Rock Deluxe (£49.99 from Babies 'R' Us★) and the Mothercare★ Walkaround Exerciser (£60) are two examples of this product.

Playpens

A playpen can be a safe and compact play area for your crawling baby and provides a convenient security zone so that, if you really have to nip out of the living room briefly, you know that he or she can't get into any trouble. Some babies may also like the feeling of the playpen being 'their' place to play, nap or simply watch your activities. On the downside, playpens take up a lot of space and not all babies take well to being hemmed in – you could find that you have spent your money on a pricey, space-occupying storage box into which you keep all manner of baby-related bits and pieces but not a baby.

If you decide to buy a playpen, do it before your baby is moving around so that you can get him or her familiar with it – there is then a better chance of it being a hit rather than a flop later on. For the same reason, if you have the space, go for a pen with a reasonably large floor area.

Types of playpen

Traditional wooden playpens have been joined in the market by brightly coloured plastic pens, multi-functional metal pens and travel cots that double up as playpens (see pages 159–61 for information on travel cots).

Wooden playpens
Pros:

✔ arguably the most attractive style of pen, simply because it generally blends in better with other furnishings (remember that even though you will be able to fold the pen away, once it is up it's likely to stay up for some time)

✔ usually has a larger floor area than other pens so more chance of it being popular with your baby.

Cons:

✘ larger floor area also means it takes up more space and can dominate the room

✘ tends to be the most expensive type (expect to pay £90 or more).

Plastic playpens
Pros:

✔ wipe-clean and easy to maintain

✔ tends to be the least expensive type of 'permanent' pen, at around £65.

Cons:

✔ can be a garish-looking piece of equipment to have semi-permanently up in your home.

Multi-functional metal pens
Pros:

✔ versatile – these pens are made up of panels that you can rearrange as either a hexagonal or rectangular pen or have as a fire surround, room divider or barrier at the bottom of the stairs (try the Baby Dan★ Babyden, £89.99 from Babies 'R' Us★ or Mothercare★)

✔ usually has a gate so you don't have to bend over to lift your baby out.

Cons:

✘ its multi-functionality is an attraction, but think about how often, realistically, you will actually rearrange it and use it for purposes other than as a playpen. You may not need a room divider, bottom-of-the-stairs barrier or a fireguard, and it may be that a simpler playpen, or the multi-functionality of a travel cot (see below), will suit your needs better.

Travel cots

Pros:

✔ cot or playpen – you choose what suits you when you need it
✔ easy to fold and store away
✔ one of the cheapest options (there is a reasonable choice around the £50 mark).

Cons:

✘ these have mesh sides, which your baby can't see through as easily as bars, so may be less appealing
✘ lack of bars also means less support for pulling up from sitting
✘ playpen floor space tends to be quite limited.

Buying tip

A removable floor pad or mattress is preferable to one that is fixed because it makes cleaning much easier.

Safety watch

- *Don't put anything in the playpen that your baby can use as a lever or step to climb out.*
- *Don't tie anything across the top as this could be a strangulation hazard.*
- *Regularly check the pen for holes in the sides or in the floor padding.*
- *Don't use the pen if it is damaged.*
- *Don't leave your child unattended in the pen unless you really have to.*

Toilet training

The trials and tribulations of toilet training may seem a long way off but they will be with you before you know it. It's hard to say when is a good time to begin toilet training – each child is different and putting a child under pressure to use a potty when he or she isn't ready will put you both under unnecessary stress. As a rough guide, a realistic time to start toilet training is at about two to two-and-a-half years old. Some parents start earlier if their child shows signs of interest, but 18 months is the earliest age to consider it. Years ago it was common practice to start toilet training at a far earlier stage than it is now (there are reports that at the beginning of the 20th century it was quite normal for the process to start at three months!). Parents and children then had practical reasons to toilet train as early as possible – with uncomfortable nappies (compounded by a lack of central heating) and poor washing facilities playing a large part. How long it took to complete the process is another matter – starting early is no indication of the age at which a child will be fully toilet trained. Thankfully, modern parents and babies have the luxury of being able to be more relaxed about the whole business. In practice, however, comparing progress with other parents and possibly being put under pressure by relatives and even nurseries or playgroups can cause toilet-training anxiety in even the most laid-back parents.

What you need

A potty is the standard item of toilet-training equipment. You'll need one or two of these. As well as potties of various sorts, you can buy a range of other toilet-training aids, from child-sized toilet-seat adaptors to washable or disposable training pants and, for night-time training, protective sheets. Books on toilet training aimed at toddlers are widely available too. As a general rule, however, it's worth starting off with the basics and seeing how you get on from there – lots of toddlers will do just fine with a standard potty, a toilet and not much else apart from a willingness to succeed.

Potties

If you are new to potties you might be surprised at the range of different types out there. Manufacturers just haven't been able to leave the standard potty alone on the shelf, and have come up with a plethora of potties (or 'toilet-training systems') with knobs on and prices to match. Not all the modern potty additions are gimmicks – some may appeal to you and to your child and could possibly help toilet training run more smoothly. But all the potties listed below will do the job well enough; the differences are largely down to personal preference and how much you are willing to pay.

Types of potty
As with many other baby products, potties range from the simple and straightforward to the gimmicky.

Standard potties
These are simple, moulded pieces of plastic, usually with children's motifs on the front, a splash guard and a slightly raised back. Expect to pay £4–5 for a basic potty from a nursery store. Devoid of 'added extras', a potty like this may suit your needs cheaply and perfectly well.

Toilet-seat adaptors
Fitting on top of the main toilet seat, these adapt the seat so it is suitable for small bottoms. Generally they are made either from moulded rigid plastic, resembling the top section of a potty but with a rim to rest over the toilet seat (roughly the same price as a standard potty) or, for a comfier sit, from vinyl-covered padded material

(these cost £10–15, depending on whether there are extras such as handles and a back-rest – The Great Little Trading Company★ sells one at the top end of the price range). If your child shows more of an interest in the toilet than the potty, one of these could be worth a try.

Potty chairs

Basically a stubby chair with a central removable potty bowl, these provide more back and side support than a standard potty and may encourage some children to sit for longer. Expect to pay £10 or so. A bit more expensive but based on a similar idea are potties shaped like a mini toilet, with a flip-up lid and removable bowl.

Convertible/multi-use potties

These can be used as either a potty or, with the base section removed, as a toilet-seat adaptor. The base can usually also be used as a handy step-stool, making it easier for your child to climb on to the toilet. The main advantage of these potties is that they are versatile so adapt to the needs of your child at different stages. He or she can use the potty at the beginning of toilet training, the toilet-seat adaptor after further progress, and can carry on with the step-stool when using the toilet as normal but still needing an extra lift up. Expect to pay £10–18 for a convertible potty. Extras may include a flip-up toilet-style lid to make the potty appear more grown-up.

Portable/travel potties

Some children don't like using unfamiliar toilets or going to the toilet in unfamiliar places (e.g. the bushes in the park). Likewise, some parents would rather their child used their own potty or toilet-seat adaptor when out and about. A travel potty can be useful in these circumstances. Tommee Tippee produces a lightweight travel potty that folds away neatly and which you line with a liner when your child needs to use it. It is available from Mothercare★ and other nursery stores for around £7, plus £2.50 for a pack of ten liners – if you use this kind of potty regularly, however, the cost of the liners can make it expensive. You can also buy the Toodle-Loo foldaway seat which folds up neatly in sections and is handy if you are concerned about hygiene in public toilets – try the shopping section of **www.travellingwithchildren.co.uk** or The Great Little Trading Company★.

Potty gimmicks

There are all sorts of ways to encourage children to use the potty, but an obvious one is to make using the potty so rewarding that children just can't resist it. Needless to say, potty manufacturers have devised potties designed to do just that. As an example, the Easy Learn potty by Bruin (£14.99 from Babies 'R' Us★) has 'tinkle targets' inside to help with aim, and a reward system with stickers and a calendar to encourage and monitor progress. JoJo Maman Bébé★ sells a musical potty trainer seat for £24.99 which makes flushing as well as musical sounds. Of course, your child doesn't need potties like this and will learn without one – but they can provide a bit of temporary fun.

If you have a little boy, the Weeman toilet trainer may be of interest – it isn't a potty but a plastic mini-urinal that clips on to the toilet seat so that little boys can wee at a convenient height for them. Contact Peppercorn Trading★ for stockists.

All-round potty buying guide

- Make sure edges are gently curved for comfort and easy cleaning.
- Check that any removable parts can be slotted in and out easily (anything with a jerky movement could cause you to splash the waste).
- Think about where you will be washing the potty out – if your basin is on the small side, a bulky potty may be difficult to fit in to rinse properly, so choose a smallish potty or one with a removable interior.
- If you have a boy, check that the potty has a reasonably high 'splash guard' (a raised section at the front).
- Let your child choose the potty if possible – he or she will feel important and will be keener to use it.
- Hold the potty to get a sense of how easy it will be to carry – you'll probably be carrying a full potty from room to room so will need easy-to-hold sides or handles.
- A high back can make it more comfortable if your child likes to use the potty as a sort of chair.

Training pants

When your child is showing clear signs that potty training is progressing well, you may want to introduce training pants into the process. They are not absolutely necessary and many parents progress straight from buying nappies to buying ordinary pants, with only a few accidents along the way. Training pants – particularly disposables – are, however, a popular toilet training aid. The idea is that your child gets used to the action of pulling pants up and down when he or she wants to go to the toilet, but there is the added security of absorbent material in the pants to cope with accidents.

There are two types of training pants – washable and disposable. Washable pants are more economical, especially if full toilet training seems to be dragging on. You can expect to pay around £5 for a pack containing two pairs of basic training pants. 'Luxury' washable training pants cost more but, since the idea is to use them for a relatively short period of time, the extra expense seems unnecessary. Disposables are more convenient in that you don't have to do any washing. They are more expensive than nappies – Huggies 'Pull Ups', for example, cost about 30p each. The main disadvantage with this type of training pants, apart from the expense, is that some children can end up using them like nappies because they won't feel the discomfort of wetness in the way that children using the less absorbent washables will. There is therefore an argument that these can extend the toilet training process rather than help to complete it. That said, many parents happily buy them because of their convenience.

Bear in mind that there is no point in using training pants before your child has a desire to use the potty or toilet and still seems unperturbed about 'soiling' him- or herself. You will be doing a lot of extra washing or spending extra money on disposable pants when this could be avoided.

> 66 When Tom was coming out of nappies I bought loads of ordinary pants with his favourite characters on – mainly Thomas the Tank Engine and Buzz Lightyear – and because he was so proud of them and didn't want to get them wet, I'm sure that helped and he was toilet trained within a few weeks. 99
>
> Nina, mother of Tom, age 4

Protective bedding

Your child is bound to wet the bed on numerous occasions once he or she stops using nappies at night. You'll want to be able to protect the mattress and change the bedding in the middle of the night quickly and easily. A range of protective sheets and covers is widely available both from nursery stores and department stores. Protective bedding has moved on from effective but uncomfortable, sweaty vinyl sheets (although you can still get these). More comfy bedding is multi-layered, with perhaps a vinyl layer but with softer, highly absorbent materials on top. A wet bed protection mat, as opposed to a protective sheet, can be very practical because it lies on top of a standard sheet so you can remove it without having to remake the bed (Urchin★ sells one for £12.95, and JoJo Maman Bébé★ sells one with 'wings' that fit under the mattress for £17.99).

Night-time training tip

When your child stops using nappies at night, keep at hand everything you will need to change the bedding in the middle of the night. Bear in mind that not only the sheet will be wet but also his or her nightclothes and possibly the quilt or blanket too. If you keep a spare set of everything close to your child's bed, disruption will be minimised.

"We have bought a bed protection mat, which is perfect for Sam's needs at the moment. He still quite often has an afternoon nap, either on the sofa or in our bed after nursery, so I just slip it under him before he nods off. It's really convenient at night too if he wets the bed as you just whip it away."

Nesta, mother of Sam, age 3

Toilet training basics

- Start potty training only when your child shows signs of being ready.
- Dress your child in clothes he or she finds easy to remove.
- Be praising when your child uses the potty but don't scold if he or she doesn't.
- Be prepared for accidents and carry spare clothing around with you.
- If you don't seem to be getting anywhere, forget about the whole thing for a few weeks and try again at a later date.
- If the summer months are approaching, consider delaying toilet training until then as your child will be wearing less and you can just carry a spare pair of shorts and pants around with you.

Websites

Babies 'R' Us	www.babiesrus.co.uk
Baby Dan	www.babydan.com
Graco	www.graco.co.uk
The Great Little Trading Company	www.gltc.co.uk
JoJo Maman Bébé	www.jojomamanbebe.co.uk
Lindam	www.lindam.com
Mothercare	www.mothercare.co.uk
Peppercorn Trading	www.peppercorntrading.com
Travelling with Children	www.travellingwithchildren.co.uk
Urchin	www.urchin.co.uk

Growing up checklist

Item	Notes
Baby bouncer	
Baby walker	
'Play station'	
Playpen	
Travel cot (Ch 5)	
Potty/toilet-seat adaptor	
Training pants	
Protective bedding	

Chapter 9

Toys

Finding the right toys for your child is a hit-and-miss affair. No matter how much research you put into it, how many shops or catalogues you scour or other parents you get advice from, you will end up with some toys that your child plays with and others that he or she doesn't. Boxes or cupboards packed with toys that rarely see the light of day are an inevitability of modern parenthood. Depending on your child's ability to concentrate, even the popular toys may provide only a short period of entertainment before he or she moves on to something else – and every parent has witnessed (or will do) their child casting a new toy aside only to play with the box it came in or the label attached! 'Grown-up' objects such as a set of keys or the TV remote control are also likely to be far more interesting than a mere child's plaything.

Despite the lottery of buying toys that will be a success, you have more chance of getting it right at least some of the time if you familiarise yourself with the various stages of your child's development – then toys can be bought to fit in with the abilities and interests of your baby as he or she grows up. Arguably, certainly during the first year, you don't really need to buy any manufactured toys at all – you're bound to be given some and you're likely to find everything else you need to stimulate your baby around the house (see 'Making your own', page 221). On the other hand, there is a certain pleasure in choosing and buying toys for your baby so, if you are going to do it anyway, it's worth following the guidelines given here.

"Be suspicious of any toy that makes claims along the lines of 'hours of fun for your child' on the packaging – 10 minutes or so is much more likely.**"**

Chris, father of Cal, age 2

Matching toys to your baby's development

Choose toys appropriate to your baby's age. Although all babies are different and some will react badly to or take little notice of a toy that another may like, the list below should help you make some good choices. Some toys will be multi-activity so you won't necessarily have to buy a separate toy for each characteristic. Remember too that a toy your baby may dislike or be disinterested in one week may prove fascinating if it is reintroduced a couple of weeks later, so don't cast aside toys that appear to have been rejected straightaway. Bear in mind that you don't have to have the latest 'all-singing, all-dancing' electronic baby toys – the classics (such as stacking towers, balls and building blocks) have remained popular for so long for good reason.

Birth to three months

Babies' hearing is better developed than their eyesight in the early weeks, and they will respond to noise and music. Your baby will first notice light and contrasting colours, particularly black against white, then move on to colourful shapes and clearly defined patterns as well as moving objects. He or she will learn to focus more as time goes on. Babies can open and close their hands from birth, then start to notice their fingers and, after about two or three months, begin to recognise that certain things happen when they move their hands. At this stage, they will start reaching out for objects.

Toys to consider:

- mobiles – particularly musical ones and those with patterns or objects that face your baby when he or she is lying in the cot
- toys with in-built mirrors – your baby won't be able to recognise him- or herself until nearly two years old, but will be fascinated by the reflections in the mirror
- brightly coloured, noisy rattles
- toys with high-contrast patterns such as simple faces.

Tip
A new baby's eyes can only focus on near objects, so hold your face about 30 centimetres from his or hers.

" We made our own mobile when Jesse was a baby. We knew that babies like contrasting colours so we made one with black and white patterns and shapes painted on to card. We also turned our triangular clothes-drying rack into a baby gym by hanging interesting bits and pieces down from the rungs and putting Jesse to lie underneath. "

Simon, father of Jesse, age 4

Three to six months

By this age babies are becoming better at reaching out for, grasping and holding objects, and may even be able to move them from one hand to the other. Their hands and the things they can hold will be explored with lips and tongue. They can sit with some support, can follow a moving object well and will look around for the source of sounds.

Toys to consider:

- baby gym or activity arch with a good selection of toy attachments to bash and swipe at
- baby 'nest' (a textile-covered inflatable ring) or play mat with different textures, flaps and squeaks
- soft toys with interesting textures and chewable attachments (but see 'Phthalates in toys' box, page 225)
- easy-to-grip plastic balls with sounds inside.

" Never buy soft toys! You're bound to be given loads anyway and my children rarely played with them. They might have one or two favourites but the rest of the pile gets ignored. "

Cassie, mother of Kane, 5 and Ceri, 3

Six to nine months

By now, babies' coordination can have developed enough for them to be able to strike an object (such as a drum) with some control, and they will enjoy hitting one object against another. Your baby will be learning that he or she is the one in control of some activities and can choose when to start and when to stop. Babies of this age will also start to explore objects properly with their hands and fingers as well as with their mouths.

Toys to consider:

- musical instrument toys, especially drums
- toys that 'react' if you press a button or push a lever
- toys with flaps or lids that can be opened and closed.

Nine to twelve months

Babies are more mobile now – they are pulling themselves up, crawling or beginning to walk. They may be starting to get interested in playthings that help with their mobility and toys that they can move along themselves. Their fingers are more dextrous and they can manipulate smaller objects than they could before. Your baby will know that if a toy has fallen it will be somewhere on the floor, and he or she will be interested in finding 'hidden' objects.

Toys to consider:

- if your baby is mobile, simple push-along toys such as chunky, easy-to-hold vehicles
- balls
- push-along baby walker
- toys your baby can play with in the bath – including items such as plastic cups as well as manufactured toys designed for the bath.

"Buy some balls. They have been a constant plaything for all three of my boys from as soon as they could reach out and pat one, to learning to kick and catch, to playing proper football. "

Stacia, mother of Sebastian, 2, George, 5 and Daniel, 8

Twelve to eighteen months

Babies of this age may start to put bits of objects together or take them apart and will find pleasure in knocking things down. Their fingers are dextrous enough to put shapes into holes, their limbs are much more coordinated and they will be 'getting into everything'. They can point at objects when asked.

Toys to consider:

- shape sorters
- stacking towers

- simple sit-on riding toys
- wooden puzzles with shaped pieces to match with shapes on the board
- stiff board books, the pages of which your baby can turn by him- or herself.

Books

It's never too early to start looking at books with your baby. Even when too young to understand what you are saying, he or she will enjoy hearing your voice. The best first books to show your baby are those with simple pictures of familiar objects in bold, bright colours, and with no or minimal text. Once your baby is seven to nine months, he or she may start to appreciate your reading very simple stories. Research has shown that babies who are encouraged to play with books from about nine months of age go on to do better at school.

" Books are the main thing that my two have shown an interest in right from early on. Stiff board books rather than fabric books are best, especially ones with photographs. Books you can attach to the pushchair are useful too – Stella still looks at hers even though it's now very tatty. "

Theo, mother of Stella, 2 and Leonie, 4

Eighteen to twenty-four months

By this stage toddlers are more proficient at building and sorting. They may show an interest in 'make-believe' games involving dolls, animals and vehicles. Your child will be keen on playing outside on simple playground equipment, and he or she may also start to want to make things.

Toys to consider:

- dolls and their paraphernalia such as mini buggies and bottles
- child-sized ride-along cars and trucks
- a first train set

- building blocks
- playdough
- matching games.

"One of the best things we ever bought was a play tent. It folds up flat so doesn't take up space and, from when they were crawling, our boys have always loved it for imaginary games."

Carlos, father of Emile, 4 and Joe, 3

Making your own

You can use all manner of everyday household items to keep your baby amused. The following are some suggestions.

- **Bell mittens** – firmly sew a bell on to each of a pair of brightly coloured mittens or scratch mittens (see page 28). Your baby will look to see where the bell sound is coming from and will soon start to associate it with the movement of his or her hands. Suitable from the age of six weeks.
- **Mirror** – attach a small mirror to a mobile above the cot or, later on (from three to six months), place a larger, unbreakable mirror inside the cot so that your baby can see his or her face and movements. From the age of about six months, you can sit with your baby and talk about your reflections in a larger mirror.
- **Shakers** – put dried pulses, coins and beads in different grippable containers with screw-top lids. (Make sure these are plastic and not made from any breakable material such as glass, and that the tops are very firmly screwed on.) Your baby will be interested in the different noises the shakers make. Suitable from three months.
- **Pots, pans and wooden spoons** – you don't have to buy drums or other toy musical instruments. Kitchen utensils can make even more noise so have the potential for more fun. Suitable from six months.
- **'Discovery' box** – set aside a box in which to put all manner of household items that are safe for your baby to play with. Make

sure there are no small removable parts (see 'Ensuring safety' box, page 224). You could include items such as textile off-cuts, plastic cups and spoons to bang together, an old TV remote control or empty video boxes. Change the items regularly so your baby or toddler knows that his or her box might always contain something new. Suitable from eight months.

Where to buy

High-street stalwarts such as **Woolworths★**, **Argos★** and larger branches of **Boots★** and **Mothercare★** are excellent for good-value toys. **Ikea★** also has a simple but appealing range. The toy departments at large department stores, independent toy shops and specialist toy chains such as the **Early Learning Centre★** will have a more varied selection. Mail-order companies such as **Urchin★** and **The Great Little Trading Company★** also have interesting toy ranges. It is also worth looking at the websites or mail-order catalogues of the following specialist toy companies for more out-of-the-ordinary and innovative products.

- **Hamleys★** – lots of classic toys plus a reasonable selection of current ranges.
- **Krucial Kids★** – educational toys, particularly for pre-schoolers.
- **Letterbox★** – a wide range of tasteful toys for babies and older children, including outdoor toys and a selection of unusual 'pop-up' and 'stacking' toys for babies.
- **Tridias★** – Online branch of a small chain of toy shops selling quality toys from makes such as Galt and Brio. A notable absence of TV/cinema-themed products.

> **"**I've always found jumble sales are really good places for buying toys. You're not spending much so it doesn't matter if you make mistakes. There are always loads of baby toys in nearly new condition – probably because parents want to get rid of all the stuff their children have ignored.**"**
>
> Catrin, mother of Owen, 3 and Robbie, 5

Toy libraries

There are toy libraries all over the UK where you can try out and take toys home with you, and these can be excellent places to visit with your baby (or, more likely, toddler). You can use them to test out a range of products on your child before you buy. Contact the National Association of Toy and Leisure Libraries (NATLL)* for details. NATLL produces an annual *Good Toy Guide*, which gives 'Gold' and 'Silver' awards for particularly innovative and imaginative toy designs; toys are also rated for their suitability for children with special needs.

Toy safety

Most toys on the market today are carefully made and safe to play with. Manufacturers have to conform to strict Europe-wide safety standards. But toys can still be hazardous if you don't take care over what you give your child. Heed the following advice.

Buying toys

- To be quite sure of safety, get your toys from a retailer with a good reputation for toys or buy only recognised brand names.
- Follow the age recommendations on the packaging – they are there for a reason. Most are intended to give you a guide to the toy's 'fun factor' suitability for children of specific ages, but any warning stating that a toy is unsuitable for children under three, for example, must be taken seriously as this indicates that the toy may be unsafe for younger children because of small parts.
- Look for the '**Lion mark**' – this is a mark of quality and safety used by manufacturers who are members of the British Toy and Hobby Association★ – the main toy trade association in the UK.
- The '**CE**' mark is another symbol you may see on toy packaging – this is a mandatory mark that must appear on toys sold within the EU and shows that toys conform to EU laws and can be sold throughout the EU (although the mark does not mean the toy has been independently tested for safety). Be wary of products that are 'toy-like' but don't have this mark (novelties,

for example) – they may not be safe for young children to play with.

- Take special care buying second-hand toys and check for broken or small, loose parts (see pages 18–20 for general advice about buying second-hand).
- Once you have bought a toy, dispose of the packaging carefully – although fascinating to young children, it could harbour unseen hazards such as staples or sharp wire. If you let your child play with the packaging, inspect it carefully first.

Caring for toys

- Use a toy box – toys lying on the floor are a serious tripping hazard.
- Throw away broken or partially broken toys.
- Keep batteries out of the reach of children and don't mix them – new batteries can make the older ones very hot.

Ensuring safety

- Remove bulky toys or activity centres from the cot as soon as your child can stand, as they can provide a foothold for climbing out.
- Make sure any toys attached to the cot are on a very short piece of string, otherwise they could be a strangulation risk.
- Keep very furry soft toys away from your baby – the fur could be a choking hazard. (The official guidance relating to 'long fibres' is that these toys shouldn't be played with by children under 18 months, and wording to this effect should appear on the label. Many manufacturers, however, use the more general recommendation of 'not for children under three' – see next point.)
- Check that the eyes, noses, bells and other trinkets on soft toys are firmly attached and remove any ribbons. Objects that are small enough for babies to put in their mouths are regarded as a choking risk until the age of about three, when children have less need to explore things with their mouths.
- Keep toys for older children separate from those for younger children.

Phthalates in toys

In recent years there has been some concern about phthalates – chemicals that have been widely used by manufacturers to soften plastic products, including plastic toys. Tests on animals have linked some phthalates with kidney and testicle damage as well as with cancer. Research has shown that phthalates can migrate from plastic toys into saliva, when children put toys in their mouths, for example. As far back as 1998, Consumers' Association was pressing for toy manufacturers to avoid using the chemical, in order to allay consumer fears – this despite government research which concluded there was no cause for concern and that there was no evidence that safety limits regarding the phthalates content of plastics were being breached. By 1999 independent safety experts were warning that parents should limit the time babies spend chewing on certain teething rings. In 2001, the EU agreed a temporary ban on phthalates in products intended to be sucked or chewed by children under three – including teething rings and dummies. At the time of writing the ban is still in force. Some manufacturers also operate a voluntary ban on phthalates in all toys aimed at children under three, not just those products that babies and small children are more likely to suck and chew. There is no regulation for the use of phthalates in toys for children over three which children may still put in their mouths.

Websites

Argos	www.argos.co.uk
Boots	www.boots.com
British Toy and Hobby Association	www.btha.co.uk
Early Learning Centre	www.elc.co.uk
The Great Little Trading Company	www.gltc.co.uk
Hamleys	www.hamleys.co.uk
Ikea	www.ikea.co.uk
Krucial Kids	www.krucialkids.com
Letterbox	www.letterbox.uk.com
Mothercare	www.mothercare.co.uk
National Association of Toy and Leisure Libraries	www.natll.org.uk
Tridias	www.tridias.co.uk
Urchin	www.urchin.co.uk
Woolworths	www.woolworths.co.uk

Addresses and websites

Addresses

Argos
Tel (customer services): 0870
600 3030
Website: www.argos.co.uk

Asda
Tel (customer services): 0500
100 055 (call to find out whether
an Asda near you has a George
Babyshop)
Website: www.asda.co.uk

B&Q
(Telephone nearest store for
stock information)
Website: www.diy.com

Babies 'R' Us
Tel (customer services): 0800
038 8889
Website: www.babiesrus.co.uk

The Baby Catalogue
(Online and mail-order catalogue)
Perfectly Happy People Ltd
37 Rothschild Road
Chiswick
London W4 5HT
Tel: 0870 122 0215;
0870 607 0545 (order line)
Website:
www.thebabycatalogue.com

Baby Dan
5 Duke Street
Southport PR8 1SE
Tel: (01704) 537843 (call for
details of product stockists)
Website: www.babydan.com

Baby Echoes
349 Hungerford Road
Crewe
Cheshire CW1 5EZ
Tel: (01270) 255201
Website: www.babyechoes.co.uk

Baby Planet
(Online only)
60 Melbourne Road
Clacton-on-Sea
Essex CO15 3HZ
Tel: (01255) 470314
Website: www.baby-planet.co.uk

Bambino Mio
(Online and mail-order catalogue)
12 Stavely Way
Brixworth
Northampton NN6 9EU
Tel: (01604) 883777
Website: www.bambino.co.uk

Beaming Baby
(Online and mail-order catalogue)
Unit 1, Place Barton Farm
Moreleigh
Totnes
Devon TQ9 7JN
Tel: 0800 034 5672
Website: www.beamingbaby.com

The Better Baby Sling
47 Brighton Road
Watford WD24 5HN
Tel: (01923) 444442
Website:
www.betterbabysling.co.uk

Blooming Marvellous
(Online and mail-order catalogue)
2nd Floor
1 The Broadway
Surbiton KT6 7DQ
Tel: 0870 751 8966
Website:
www.bloomingmarvellous.co.uk
10 shops: in Bath, Bluewater,
Chester, Cobham, London,
Manchester, Marlow, Richmond,
St Albans and Winchester

Boots
Tel (customer services):
0845 070 8090
Website: www.boots.com

**British Association of Nursery
and Pram Retailers**
90 St Brannock's Road
Ilfracombe
Devon EX34 8EG
Tel: 0870 410 6114

**British Toy and Hobby
Association**
80 Camberwell Road
London SE5 0EG
Tel: 020-7701 7271
Website: www.btha.co.uk

Charlie Crow
(Online and mail-order catalogue)
Unit 2
Crabtree Close
Fenton
Stoke-on-Trent ST4 2SW
Tel: (01782) 417133
Website: www.charliecrow.com

Cheeky Rascals
(Mail-order catalogue)
1 Stone Barn
The Brows
Farnham Road
Liss
Hampshire GU33 6JG
Tel: 0870 873 2600
Website: www.cheekyrascals.co.uk
(no online ordering)

Child Accident Prevention Trust
4th Floor
18–20 Farringdon Lane
London EC1R 3HA
Tel: 020-7608 3828

Child Safety Centre
23A/B Mullacreevie Park
Killylea Road
Armagh BT60 4BA
Tel: 028-3752 6521
Website: www.capt.org.uk

Clippasafe
Lanthwaite Road
Clifton
Nottingham NG11 8LD
Tel: 0115-921 1899 (call for
details of product stockists)
Website: www.clippasafe.co.uk

Cotton Bottoms
7–9 Water Lane Industrial Estate
Water Lane
Storrington
West Sussex RH20 3XX
Tel: 0870 777 8899
Website:
www.cottonbottoms.co.uk

Disabled Living Centres Council
Redbank House
4 St Chad's Street
Manchester M8 8QA
Tel: 0161-834 1044
Website: www.dlcc.co.uk

Disabled Living Foundation
380–384 Harrow Road
London W9 2HU
Tel: 020-7289 6111 (enquiries);
0845 130 9177 (helpline)
Textphone: 020-7432 8009
Website: www.dlf.org.uk

Dorel
Hertsmere House
Shenley Road
Borehamwood
Hertfordshire WD6 1TE
Tel: 020-8236 7325
Website: www.dorel.com,
www.maxi-cosi.com

Early Learning Centre (ELC)
Head Office:
South Marston Park
Swindon SN3 4TJ
Orders:
Early Learning Direct
PO Box 4020
Manchester M99 1DA
Tel (customer services):
0870 535 2352
Website: www.elc.co.uk

Food Standards Agency (FSA)
Aviation House
125 Kingsway
London WC2B 6NH
Tel: 020-7276 8000
Website: www.food.gov.uk

Foundation for the Study of Infant Deaths (SIDS)
Artillery House
11–19 Artillery Row
London SW1P 1RT
Tel: 0870 787 0554 (helpline);
0870 787 0885 (general)
Website: www.sids.org.uk/fsid

Graco
1st Floor
900 Pavilion Drive
Northampton NN4 7RG
Tel: 0870 909 0501 (call for details of product stockists)
Website: www.graco.co.uk

The Great Little Trading Company
(Online and mail-order catalogue)
35 Adam & Eve Mews
London W8 6UG
Tel (customer services): 0870 850 6000
Website: www.gltc.co.uk

Green Baby
(Online and mail-order catalogue)
Unit 2Q/R, Leroy House
436 Essex Rd
London N1 3QP
Tel: 0870 240 6894
Website: www.greenbabyco.com
Shops: 345 Upper Street, London N1 0PD (tel: 020-7359 7037) *and* 5 Elgin Crescent, London W11 2JA (tel: 020-7792 8140)

Grobag
(Online and mail-order catalogue)
Fusion House
Lower Union Road
Kingsbridge
Devon TQ7 1EF
Tel: (01548) 854444
Website: www.grobag.com

Halfords
Tel (customer services): (01527) 513555
Website: www.halfords.com
(for safety reasons car seats can only be bought in-store, although they can be viewed online)

Hamleys
188–196 Regent Street
London W1R 6BT
Tel: 0870 333 2455
Website: www.hamleys.co.uk

Homebase
Tel (customer services):
0845 077 8888
Website: www.homebase.co.uk

Huggababy
19–21 The Prya Centre
Talgarth
Brecon
Powys LD3 0DS
Tel: (01874) 711629
Website: www.huggababy.co.uk

Ikea
(Telephone nearest store for
stock information)
Website: www.ikea.co.uk

Index
Tel (customer services):
0870 264 4444
Website:www.index.co.uk

Jack Horner
PO Box 1448
Rugby CV23 8ZE
Tel: (01788) 891890 (call for
details of product stockists)
Website: www.jack-horner.co.uk

Jané
Johnston Prams and Buggies Ltd
Unit 6 Trench Park
Trench Road
Mallusk
Newtonabbey
BT36 4TY
Tel: 028-9084 9045
Website: www.jane.es
(worldwide);
www.johnstonprams.co.uk (UK)

John Lewis
Tel (customer services): 0845
604 9049
Website: www.johnlewis.com

JoJo Maman Bébé
Customer Services:
Oxwich Road
Reevesland Park
Newport NP19 4PU
Tel: 0870 160 8820 (customer
services); 0870 241 0560 (order
line)
Website:
www.jojomamanbebe.co.uk
Shop: 3 Ashbourne Parade
1259 Finchley Road, London
NW11 0AD (tel: 020-8731 8961)
Warehouse sale shop: Oxwich
Road, Reevesland Park, Newport
NP19 4PU (tel: (01633) 294460)

Kays
Tel (customer services):
0870 151 0541
Website: www.kaysnet.com

Kiddicare
1182 Lincoln Road
Werrington
Peterborough PE4 6LA
Tel: (01733) 579175
Website: www.kiddicare.com

Kidsense
Foxlands Farm
Croft Road
Cosby
Leicestershire LE9 1SG
Tel: (01455) 550600
Website: www.kidsense.co.uk

Krucial Kids
(Online and mail-order catalogue)
Unit 11
Enterprise Way
Flitwick
Bedfordshire MK45 5BW
Tel: (01525) 722740
Website: www.krucialkids.com

La Leche League
PO Box 29
West Bridgford
Nottingham NG2 7NP
Tel: 0845 120 2918 (general
breast-feeding information and
support helpline)
Website: www.laleche.org.uk

Letterbox
(Online and mail-order catalogue)
Tregony Business Park
Tregony
Truro
Cornwall TR2 5TL
Tel: 0870 600 7878
Website: letterbox.co.uk

Lilliput
255 Queenstown Road
London SW8 3NP
Tel: 020-7720 5554
Website: www.lilliput.com
(no online ordering)
4 shops: in Battersea (see above),
Wimbledon (tel: 020-8542 3542),
Harrogate (tel: (01423) 524040)
and Inverness (tel: (01463)
715565)

Lindam
Hornbeam Square West
Hornbeam Park
Harrogate
North Yorkshire HG2 8PA
Tel: 0870 111 8118 (call for
details of product stockists)
Website: www.lindam.com

Little Green Earthlets
(Online and mail-order catalogue)
Units 17
Silveroak Farm
Waldron
Heathfield
East Sussex TN71 0RS
Tel: (01825) 873301
Website: www.earthlets.co.uk

Littlewoods
Tel (customer services): 08457
979797
Website: www.littlewoods.com

Lullabys
Coton Hill
Shrewsbury SY1 2LD
Tel: (01743) 233233
Website: www.lullabys.co.uk

Mamas & Papas
Colne Bridge Road
Huddersfield
HD5 0RH
Tel: 0870 830 7700
Website:
www.mamasandpapas.co.uk

Marks and Spencer
Tel (customer services):
0845 302 1234
Website:
www.marksandspencer.co.uk

Mini Boden
(Online and mail-order catalogue)
Customer Services:
Boden
Meridian West
Meridian Business Park
Leicester LE19 1PX
Tel: 0845 677 5000
Website: www.boden.co.uk

Mischief Kids
*('Real world' shop and online
ordering)*
20 Market Street
Leigh
Lancashire WN7 1DS
Tel: (01942) 607222
Website:
www.mischiefkids.co.uk

Mothercare
Tel (customer services):
0845 330 4030
Website: www.mothercare.co.uk

**National Association of Nappy
Services (NANS)**
(call the number below for postal
address of the current chair of
NANS)
Tel: 0121-693 4949
Website:
www.changeanappy.co.uk

**National Association of Toy and
Leisure Libraries (NATLL)**
68 Churchway
London NW1 1LT
Tel: 020-7255 4600
Scotland office
1st Floor
Gilmerton Community Centre
4 Drum Street
Edinburgh EH17 8QG
Tel: 0131-664 2746
Website: www.natll.org.uk

**National Childbirth Trust
(NCT)**
Alexandra House
Oldham Terrace
Acton
London W3 6NH
Tel: 0870 444 8707 (enquiry line
– call for details of your local
NCT branch); 0870 444 8708
(breast-feeding support line)
Website: www.nctpregnancyand
babycare.com

The Natural Mat Company
('Real world' shop, online and mail-order catalogue)
99 Talbot Road
London W11 2AT
Tel: 020-7985 0474
Website: www.naturalmat.com

Nippers
Little Porters
Porters Lane
Fordham Heath
Colchester CO3 9TZ
Tel: (01206) 243626
Website: www.nippers.co.uk
9 outlets: in Canterbury,
Chessington, Colchester, Milton
Keynes, Norwich, Royston,
Rugby, Taunton and Worcester

Peppercorn Trading
368 Alexandra Park Road
London N22 7BD
Tel: 020-8888 9692
Website:
www.peppercorntrading.com

Prince Lionheart
Suite 252
2 Lansdowne Row
London W1J 6HL
Tel: 0870 766 5197
Website:
www.princelionheart.co.uk

Rabbitts
(Mail-order catalogue)
13 Wych Elms
Park Street
St Albans
Hertfordshire AL2 2AR
Tel: (01727) 768191
Website: www.rabbitts.com

Redinap
PO Box 6632
Birmingham B37 6DD
Tel: 0121-788 0300 (call for
details of product stockists)
Website: www.redinap.com

Ricability
30 Angel Gate
326 City Road
London EC1V 2PT
Tel: 020-7427 2460
Website: www.ricability.org.uk

Sainsbury's
Tel (customer services): 0800
636262
Website: www.sainsburys.com

Silver Cross
Nesfield House
Broughton Hall
Skipton
North Yorkshire BD23 3AN
Tel: (01756) 702412
Website: www.silvercross.co.uk

Snugger
PO Box 570
Cheam
Sutton
Surrey SM2 7LE
Tel: 020-8224 8766
Website: www.snuggeruk.com

Starchild
Unit 17/18
Oak Business Centre
Ratcliffe Road
Sileby
Leicester LE12 7PU
Tel: (01509) 817600 (order line)
Website:
www.starchildshoes.co.uk

Stokke
3 The Old Stables
Shredding Green Farm
Langley Park Road
Iver
Buckinghamshire SL0 9QS
Tel: (01753) 655873 (call for
details of product stockists)
Website: www.stokke.com

Sunday Best
*('Real world' shop and online
ordering)*
115 Adnitt Road
Northampton NN1 4NQ
Tel: (01604) 470168
Website: www.sundaybest
christening.com

Tesco
Tel (customer services):
0800 505555
Website: www.tesco.com

Tomy
PO Box 20
Totton
Hampshire SO40 3YF
Tel: 023-80 66 2600 (call for
details of product stockists)
Website: www.tomy.co.uk

Tridias
(Online and mail-order catalogue)
The Buffer Depot
Badminton Road
Acton Turville
Gloucestershire GL9 1HE
Tel: 0870 443 1300
Website: www.tridias.co.uk
5 shops: in Bath, Dartington,
London (Kensington and
Richmond) and Plymouth

Twinkle Twinkle
(Online and mail-order catalogue)
Beggars Hill Road
Lands End
Twyford
Berkshire RG10 0UB
Tel: 0118-934 2120
Website:
www.twinkleontheweb.co.uk

UK Nappy Line
Tel: (01983) 401959; (01324)
878609 (Scotland); 0845 456 2477
(Wales)
Website: www.nappyline.org.uk

Urchin
(Online and mail-order catalogue)
Freepost SCE 6264
Marlborough
Wiltshire SN8 3YY
Tel: 0870 720 3040
Website: www.urchin.co.uk

Vertbaudet
PO Box 125
Bradford BD99 4YG
Tel: 0845 270 0270
Website: www.vertbaudet.co.uk

WigWam Kids
Unit 44
Bilston Glen Industrial Estate
Dryden Road
Loanhead
Edinburgh EH20 9NZ
Tel: 0870 902 7500
Website:
www.wigwamkids.co.uk

Wilkinet
(Online and mail-order catalogue)
PO Box 20
Cardigan SA43 1JB
Tel: 0800 138 3400
Website: www.wilkinet.co.uk

Websites

Retail

www.discountbabystore.co.uk
www.ebay.co.uk
www.kidsgloriouskids.co.uk
www.kidsonthemove.co.uk
www.realcycles.com

General

www.babydirectory.com
www.babygoes2.com
www.babysurf.co.uk
www.babyworld.co.uk
www.ciao.co.uk
www.netmums.com
www.specialneedskids.co.uk
www.topoftheshops.co.uk
www.travellingwithchildren.co.uk
www.ukchildrensdirectory.com
www.ukparents.co.uk

Index

The Which? Guide to Financing Your Child's Future

Whether you are expecting your first baby or are the parent of a teenager, you are bound to be aware that bringing up children is not cheap. But, as this practical and independent financial handbook shows, you may not have to shoulder the entire burden yourself.

Financial institutions tend to worry parents with statistics about how much money they should be saving for their children. *The Which? Guide to Financing Your Child's Future* sorts the facts from the scaremongering, giving you the lowdown on what you are really up against. Packed with tips, charts and real-life case histories, the book covers:

- the cost of childcare, and sources of help
- the expenses involved in education – from school through the gap year to university
- how to help your child to get a foot on the property ladder
- the essential financial changes you should make when you become a parent, such as making a will and buying life insurance
- the best ways to save for your children
- the steps that parents and grandparents can take to minimise tax on gifts to children.

Paperback   216 x 135mm   208 pages   £10.99

Available from bookshops, and by post from
Which? Books, Freepost, PO Box 44, Hertford SG14 1SH
or phone FREE on (0800) 252100 quoting Dept BKLIST

Buy, Sell and Move House

Buying and selling houses is always stressful, and mishaps can be time-consuming as well as expensive. This bestselling guide puts you in control, explaining each stage of the process to help you steer clear of problems and minimise setbacks. Newly updated, the book explains all the necessary legal, financial and practical considerations.

Among the topics covered are:

*   deciding on the best property for your needs
*   the legal process, from exchange of contracts to completion
*   mortgage options
*   getting the best from solicitors, estate agents and other professionals
*   selling without an estate agent
*   using the Internet to buy and sell your home
*   buying a newly built house
*   valuations, surveys and doing up a property
*   how to present your home to buyers in the best light
*   how to calculate – and cut down on – moving expenses
*   organising and surviving the move.

A glossary explains many of the legal and financial terms you are likely to come across, and a separate chapter deals with the different system that operates in Scotland.
This guide does not cover flats, or property transfer in Northern Ireland.

Paperback   216 x 135mm   320 pages   £11.99

Available from bookshops, and by post from
Which? Books, Freepost, PO Box 44, Hertford SG14 1SH
or phone FREE on (0800) 252100 quoting Dept BKLIST

WHICH? BOOKS

The following titles were available as this book went to press.

General (legal, financial, practical etc)

160 Letters that Get Results	352 pages	£10.99
450 Legal Problems Solved	352 pages	£11.99
Baby Products	256 pages	£11.99
Be Your Own Financial Adviser	448 pages	£11.99
Buy, Own and Sell a Flat	352 pages	£11.99
Buy, Sell and Move House	320 pages	£11.99
Buying Property Abroad	256 pages	£10.99
Choosing a Career	192 pages	£6.99
Do Your Own Conveyancing	208 pages	£11.99
Getting the Best from your Builder	192 pages	£9.99
Getting Married	256 pages	£11.99
Living Together	208 pages	£10.99
Money M8	176 pages	£6.99
Rip Off Britain	256 pages	£5.99
Take Control of Your Pension Action Pack	48 pages	£10.99

A5 wallet with 48-page book, calculation tables and reference material

What to Do When Someone Dies	192 pages	£10.99
The Which? Book of Wiring and Lighting (hardback)	160 pages	£16.99
The Which? Computer Troubleshooter	192 pages	£12.99
Which? Way to Clean It	256 pages	£10.99
Which? Way to Drive Your Small Business	240 pages	£10.99
Which? Way to Get an eLife	272 pages	£9.99
Wills and Probate	256 pages	£11.99

The Which? Guide to:

Changing Careers	352 pages	£10.99
Computers	352 pages	£10.99
Divorce	352 pages	£11.99
Employment	352 pages	£11.99
the Energy-Saving Home	224 pages	£10.99
Financing Your Child's Future	208 pages	£10.99
Gambling	288 pages	£9.99
Giving and Inheriting	288 pages	£10.99
Going Digital	272 pages	£10.99
Help in the Home	208 pages	£9.99
Making the Most of Retirement	256 pages	£10.99
Money in Retirement	288 pages	£10.99

Money on the Internet	256 pages	£9.99
Renting and Letting	352 pages	£11.99
Starting Your Own Business	224 pages	£10.99
Working from Home	304 pages	£10.99

Health
250 Medical Questions Answered	316 pages	£10.99
Which? Medicine	512 pages	£14.99

The Which? Guide to:
Asthma and Allergies	256 pages	£11.99
Complementary Therapies	256 pages	£10.99
Counselling and Therapy	288 pages	£10.99
Managing Back Trouble	160 pages	£9.99
Managing Stress	304 pages	£10.99
Men's Health	336 pages	£9.99
Women's Health	448 pages	£10.99

Gardening
The Gardening Which? Guide to:
Growing Your Own Vegetables (hardback)	224 pages	£18.99
Patio and Container Plants	224 pages	£17.99
Small Gardens	224 pages	£12.99
Successful Perennials	224 pages	£12.99
Successful Propagation	160 pages	£12.99
Successful Pruning	240 pages	£12.99
Successful Shrubs	224 pages	£12.99

Travel/leisure
The Good Bed and Breakfast Guide	432 pages	£15.99
The Good Food Guide	816 pages	£15.99
The Good Skiing and Snowboarding Guide	352 pages	£15.99
The Which? Pub Guide	544 pages	£15.99

The Which? Guide to:
Good Hotels	544 pages	£15.99
Pub Walks in the South-East	256 pages	£10.99

Available from bookshops, and by post from:
Which? Books, Freepost, PO Box 44, Hertford SG14 1SH
or phone FREE on (0800) 252100 quoting Dept BKLIST